D1548167

Sir Adrian Boult

Overleaf: Photo Constantine, by kind permission of *Classical Music*

Sir Adrian Boult

Companion of Honour

A Tribute edited by
Nigel Simeone
and
Simon Mundy

Midas Books

In the same series of Great Performers
PAGANINI John Sugden
TOSCANINI Denis Matthews and Ray Burford
MARIA CALLAS Carla Verga

REF
ML
422
.B79
S55
Cop. 1R

First published in 1980 by
Midas Books
12 Dene Way, Speldhurst, Tunbridge Wells, Kent TN3 0NX

Compilation © Nigel Simeone, Simon Mundy 1980

All rights reserved. No part of this publication may
be reproduced, stored in a retrieval system, or transmitted
in any form or by any means, electronic, mechanical,
photocopying, recording or otherwise, without the prior permission of
Midas Books

Sir Adrian Boult, a life in music. — (Great
   performers series).
   1. Boult, *Sir* Adrian
   785′.092′4   ML422.B79

ISBN 0 85936 217 5 De-luxe limited edition 100 copies
ISBN 0 85936 212 4 Library edition

Book production by Chambers Green Ltd
Book designed by Stonecastle Graphics
Typesetting by Style Photosetting Ltd
Tunbridge Wells, Kent
Printed in Great Britain by R. J. Acford Ltd Chichester

The Editors

NIGEL SIMEONE

Nigel Simeone was born in London in 1956. He was educated at Leighton Park School, Reading and at Manchester University, graduating with an honours degree in Music. Whilst there he was active as a conductor, performing a number of little-known works especially by Eastern European composers. He is a dealer in antiquarian music and books, and also writes occasionally for *Classical Music* and other journals.

SIMON MUNDY

Simon Mundy was born in 1954 and educated at Westminster School and Manchester University. He returned to London in 1976 and took up writing. Now freelance, he writes for *Classical Music*, *The Listener* and broadcasts regularly for BBC Radio.

Acknowledgements

Apart from those who have so kindly contributed articles to this volume there are many whom we must thank: Joan Coulson of EMI Records; EMI Records for permission to reproduce photographs in their possession; the late Lawrence Tanner for access to documents and photographs; Jane Whitton, for copying Mr Tanner's material; James Robbins and Daniel Brittain-Catlin for allowing us to pillage moments from an interview which originally appeared in the *Grantite Review* (house magazine of Grant's, Westminster School); the editor and publisher of the *Gramophone* for permission to reprint the articles by Jerrold Northrop Moore and Christopher Bishop; Mrs Gwen Beckett for access to Sir Adrian's files; and finally Miss Olive Boult for much interesting information about her brother. The editors' royalties from this book will be donated to the British Musicians Sick and Pensions Society.

N.S.
S.M.

Contents

Foreword

Dr Malcolm Williamson, CBE
Master of the Queen's Music

While there is a wealth of material on Sir Adrian Boult, the subject is so rich that this new book is a valuable addition to what, even in the great man's lifetime, one might call the Boult Literature.

Some years ago, after a superb Beethoven series, inevitably capped with a cool and excellent performance of the Schubert Great C Major Symphony, I had the temerity to write to Sir Adrian saying that, in my view, the only comparable conductor of our time was Bruno Walter. If this view now needs revision, it is only because we can see that Sir Adrian is possibly even greater.

We have now, on the one hand, sufficient documentation of the early Boult performances, and, on the other hand, the modern Boult recordings with their spacious and profound readings which make it quite clear that Sir Adrian has illuminated music with unique understanding in this century.

Sir Adrian's contribution is not only of our time. He has stamped his thumbprint of excellence on musical performance with his conducting, his teaching and his writings – an insurance for the future of music.

The man of one syllable words, peculiar sophistication, subtle humour, profound understanding, exemplary professionalism and humility before music deserves celebration.

Editors' Introduction

This little book is not intended to be a biography of Sir Adrian Boult; rather, it is a collection of articles by his friends and by those who have worked closely with him. Roughly speaking, these have been arranged in chronological order, beginning with comments on his school and student days by Sir Adrian himself and by Lawrence Tanner, a lifelong friend who, sadly, died before this book went to press. In several of these articles we can see aspects of British musical life of this century illuminated by the comments of musicians whose experience goes back in one case to Hans Richter and in another to the Royal College of Music in the days when Stanford conducted the First Orchestra there. At the other end of the spectrum we have the response of the new generation of musicians, represented here by Richard Hickox. Also examined is Sir Adrian's own response to the demands of modern recording technology as described by Christopher Bishop, his producer for a number of years.

Sir Adrian's style has many individual facets which have often stimulated discussion – in particular his stick technique and his fierce defence of the old orchestral layout, with the second violins on the conductor's right. These are often referred to here and commented upon, both critically and appreciatively by several leading orchestral players. The origin of his style can, of course, be traced back to England's concert life at the turn of the century and, more importantly, his years of pilgrimage to Leipzig, where Nikisch's work with the Gewandhaus Orchestra formed much of the basis for Sir Adrian's own approach to music-making. However, it was not only Nikisch who influenced Adrian Boult: Hans Richter's Wagner and Brahms, Steinbach's Bach, and others all made their mark on this receptive young musician. Most uncommonly among conductors of international reputation, Boult has always been known for the high regard in which he is held by orchestral musicians. Paradoxically, the features that many remember about his rehearsals are his dry wit and his refusal to tolerate anything but the highest standards. What is appreciated by orchestral musicians more than anything else is his unwillingness to rehearse for a moment longer than necessary.

His ability as an orchestral trainer, especially at the BBC, was recognised internationally – to such an extent that conductors such as Toscanini, Bruno Walter, Koussevitzky and Mengelberg were happy to conduct Boult's BBC orchestra at a time when they were unwilling to conduct any other British orchestra on a regular basis. Having built up this orchestra over a period of twenty years, Sir Adrian was compulsorily retired at the age of sixty in 1950; a ruling which, for conductors at least (well-known for their near-immortality!) was demonstrably ridiculous, as Sir Adrian went on to show, spending almost thirty years of active life on the podium, generally with either the London Philharmonic Orchestra (of which he is still president) or the BBC Symphony Orchestra. Colin Bradbury has written charmingly about these later years.

Whilst his time at the BBC attracts the lion's share of the attention, his six years as principal conductor of the City of Birmingham Symphony Orchestra (1924-1930) should not be forgotten, for he built that orchestra into the full professional organisation which it has been ever since. The Birmingham critic Lyndon Jenkins has written an interesting article about this period in Boult's career – his first major conducting appointment, with an orchestra for which he retained an affection, returning for a season in 1959 as its principal conductor.

Our own memories of Boult cover most of our lives but only the Indian Summer of his own career. It is hard to forget things like his readings of the Elgar symphonies, the Great Schubert C major and perhaps, above all, performances of Vaughan Williams' *Job* (dedicated to him) and Brahms' Third Symphony at his last Proms in 1977. We hope that the memories and tributes of those writing in this book convey something of his influence on younger musicians, his consummate professionalism and, above all, the admiration and affection in which he is held by so many of his colleagues.

Nigel Simeone
Simon Mundy

Five Ashes, E. Sussex, 1980

Overleaf: Sir Adrian Boult with Yehudi Menuhin.

Photo by courtesy of EMI Ltd.

Tribute

YEHUDI MENUHIN, KBE

It is with heartfelt admiration and great joy that I join in this tribute to my dear colleague and long-standing friend, Sir Adrian Boult. I shall always think of him as one who shared his knowledge and vast experience unstintingly with the younger generations, and I shall never forget how generously and patiently he took me through Berlioz's *Symphonie Fantastique*, and how painstakingly he illustrated his elegant and economical use of the baton together with a delicate finger technique.

How often has this experience made me wish that other conductors, both young and old, who slash a bloodthirsty way through soloists and orchestras alike, their batons becoming Saladin's scimitars, would heed Sir Adrian's example. His quiet effectiveness betrays no lack of passion – he simply witholds this until he needs it. I can bear witness to that!

In the early television days, before the BBC was equipped with zoom lenses, and when cameras would appear from nowhere to peer insolently up one's nostrils, Sir Adrian suddenly found one of these mobile Cyclops glaring at him. The resultant explosion was short, magnificent and salutary, and from then on the camera knew its place.

As far as I am concerned, I have always known mine when we have been together on the platform – a little to the side, and below, and full of affection and respect.

Yehudi Menuhin

YEHUDI MENUHIN (b. 1916), the distinguished violinist, was a pupil of Adolf Busch and Enesco. He has appeared with Sir Adrian on many occasions both in concerts and on records. In 1965 he was awarded an honorary KBE.

Katharine Florence Boult, Sir Adrian's mother.   *Photo Jane Whitton*

The Years at Westminster School and Oxford

SIMON MUNDY

In April, 1901, Adrian Boult was sent to Westminster School. His house was Grant's, reputedly the oldest school boarding house in the country and still bearing the name of the family which ran it in the middle of the eighteenth century. Almost the first person he met 'up Grant's' was the son of the housemaster, Lawrence Tanner, who had already been in the school for a few terms although he was a year younger. The close friendship between the future musician and the future historian and Keeper of the Muniments of Westminster Abbey lasted all their lives, as did their correspondence. This picture of life at Westminster, Oxford and the holidays in between is built from a series of interviews, and the letters, from their parents as well as themselves, that were in the possession of Lawrence Tanner, who sadly died in November 1979, shortly after my visits. Among many claims to distinction by Lawrence Tanner was that he was the only person to attend every coronation this century.

"Lawrence Tanner was sitting next to me at lunch my first day and we sat next to each other at lunch for seven years after that. He was a half-boarder 'up Grant's' and lived with his father. He had his own bedroom – he wasn't in dormitories. He had been there for two terms." (A.C.B.)

"Mrs Boult was perfectly charming and particularly so to me. I went straight to Westminster; too young actually. My mother had died and my father wanted to keep me by him. I think she was sorry for this motherless little boy. I used to go and stay with them a lot in the school holidays. I can see her now. She was very striking looking in a black silk dress with a very high Medici collar and it suited her enormously. She was very great on stamps and she had very beautiful hands. I can see her sitting at the table playing with her stamps and licking them and so on. She was a very cultured person; took a great interest in old books and such like. Some bookseller in Liverpool always used to send her antiquarian books. She even wrote a novel, under the name of Newton Stewart, about Frederick II, called 'Son of the Emperor'.

"Adrian's father was in oil, in those early days. A curious thing called Valvoline Oil in Liverpool and when I first knew him they were living at Blundell Sands. It was rather fascinating, because you could see all the boats going along the Mersey as they came in – and the sands were wonderful. I learnt to bicycle staying with him, sticking a peg in where I fell off on the tennis lawn. The sands were so hard you could bicycle on them quite happily. His sister, Olive, used to ride in those days. I think Adrian did too but I don't remember him actually on a horse. Then Adrian's father used to come back from a day in Liverpool. They had a billiards room and he always used to retire there. He was a great billiards player. It was the time of Free Trade and Protection – he was very much a politician, so to speak. I can hear him now saying 'Take the case of Boots!' I can't tell you what happened about the 'case of Boots!'

"Then they moved to a beautiful house – the Abbey Manor in West Kirby. That was a big house and owing to the lie of the land West Kirby was entirely blotted out and you looked right across to the Welsh Hills and the Dee."   (L.E.T.)

At school Adrian Boult was to some extent relieved of the rigorous discipline of a boarding house by living in a flat on the other side of the river, 13 St Thomas's Mansions, Westminster Bridge Road.

"Of course that block has gone now, just behind St Thomas's Hospital, before you get to Lambeth Bridge; quite nice. There was a Miss Patterson, a friend of the Boults, who lived there as well; she was a secretary to Canon Barnet who lived in the cloisters. Mrs Barnet was a very alarming lady."   (L.E.T.)

Adrian Boult as a young man.   *Photo Jane Whitton*

There was nothing exceptional about Adrian Boult's attitude to lessons, as his housemaster implied in a letter to his mother in the Lent Term, 1903.

"I think that he is doing pretty well this term, but he is apt to be a bit dreamy in form and comes back with a start to everyday life and the relentless questions forced on his unwilling brain . . ."

Music was not taken particularly seriously by the school authorities even though the Headmaster, Dr Gow, was himself musical, which at least meant that boys wanting permission to attend concerts outside were likely to get a sympathetic response. However, Mr Ranalow, the music master, was less than imaginative.

"We had an annual school concert when everybody sang a Gilbert and Sullivan opera, and everybody sang the tune an octave lower. Chorus parts weren't known; nobody ever sang a bass part. And that was all that happened. I played the piano, but I didn't have any official lessons at school. There was a man named Piggott who wasn't on the staff very long – he went to Dartmouth and became second master there. He gave me a good deal of music at that time. We went to concerts together and we did harmony and counterpoint and things like that. But as a private tutor; nobody really knew he was musical, as a matter of fact." (A.C.B.)

Later in 1903, during the summer holidays spent, as usual, in Scotland, the lessons were repaid in music.

"August 4th. Adrian is in the throes of composition, writing a wedding present for Mr Piggott. It sounds rather nice to me but of course poor Mr Piggott will have the invidious task of pulling his own wedding present apart." (Florence Boult to L.E.T.)

A few days later the termly form results came through and the French prize rather surprised the recipient's mother! She wrote to Lawrence Tanner on August 15th . . .

"Wasn't Adrian lucky? Your Daddy made such ominous remarks in the reports that I quite thought Adrian would be somewhere near the bottom of the form."

Meanwhile Boult put his learning to the test the same day, as he told his friend.

"In the train there were two members of a party of emigrants and they couldn't speak a word of English and I spoke the most awful French to them . . . although I had received a prize not 6 hrs before!! I shot 2 grouse on the twelfth, or rather, to use the Punch Frenchman's expression, 'I had one brace to my bags'."

In 1904 he met Frank Schuster for the first time. Schuster was a wealthy patron of the arts who lived in Old Queen Street, just round the corner from Westminster, and his aunt was a family friend of the Boults in Liverpool.

"Frank sent me a card for a concert at the Queen's Hall which I was going to already. I was in the back row and he was in the middle of the circle so I gave away my ticket and went to sit with him. Then we

Photograph of Grant's House, Westminster School, 1908. L. to R. (seated): Ralph Tanner (housemaster), Lord Adrian, Lawrence Tanner, Adrian Boult.
Photo Jane Whitton

walked home together and after that he invited me quite often. One night a messenger boy came round with a card for dinner. It was a party of, I think, about five or six men only, the ladies came later, and there was Elgar, Theo Lierhammer, the singer, and Fritz Volbach, the conductor, who had just done 'The Apostles' at Mainz. I was fifteen! This was all just after the Elgar Festival at Covent Garden, while Elgar was staying with Frank. He had to break open the garden gate onto Birdcage Walk to get Elgar in and out, because the Press were congregating outside the front door and he wanted peace!"

That winter and for the first part of 1905 Boult was sent to South Africa to recover from a bout of illness. His parents thought he was a delicate child, which was their main reason for sending him to Westminster rather than to a more austere country boarding school. His work suffered from the time away from the classroom, but when he came back from his trip, much stronger, his future path was clear to his mother. On 17th August 1905, she wrote to Mr Tanner, the housemaster.

"It is quite evident that Adrian will never do anything that makes money and as Mr Piggott thinks that he really will be a musician the

Three views of Abbey Manor, West Kirby. *Above:* The drive. *Opposite top:* The house itself, showing the small summer house which was reputedly used as a refuge by a murderer. *Opposite bottom:* The Hall, built c.1800, though parts of the house were built much earlier.   *Photo Jane Whitton*

25

only thing is to prepare him for that thoroughly. It is slow work and meantime we think that he had better go to Oxford – for he can work at music in conjunction with – oh, – ordinary work. What is your idea of a college? We should like Christchurch or Balliol, the first preferably if it has really (and I am told it has) outlived it's evil reputation.

"I know most about Balliol and for several reasons should prefer him not being there – but they are not serious reasons, not worth writing, so that if you think it better there than the House we should be glad to know.

"Ought he to be entered at once? We want to keep him at Westminster up to the very last minute if you will have him. It is dreadful to have him growing up at all; I expect you feel the same about Lawrence."

The next term it was Lawrence Tanner who was ill and convalescing away from school. Boult's account to him of the Commemoration of Benefactors service in the school chapel (Westminster Abbey) gives an entertaining glimpse into the rivalries of the musical establishment of the time, in the persons of Mr Ranalow and Sir Frederick Bridge, the Abbey Organist.

"22nd. November, '05. Sorry you missed Commem. Perhaps you are not though. Ranalow is in high strikes about it. He was congratulated by many kind OWW [Old Westminsters], who all said 'Of course you had the help of the Abbey Choir?' and he was proud to be able to say, 'No, my good man, we did it all ourselves'. Bridge played and succeeded in tangling himself up thoroughly once or twice but we went on manfully without him. He also stopped all through one verse of the hymn (Ranalow said it was in order to make us break down) but we didn't turn a hair."

For both boys the opportunities of growing up in the centre of London were fully grasped, whether musical (Boult had season tickets for Henry Wood's Saturday and Sunday concerts at the Queen's Hall) or historical: the Abbey and Question Time at the House of Commons (preferential entry to which is an ancient school privilege). Even form friendships took on an allusive intellectual flavour:

"Four of us called ourselves the Quadruple Alliance after memories of Walpole! It was Adrian and myself and Clifton Gordon, whose father had St John's, the church in the Waterloo Road and was a governor of the Old Vic. He'd helped to found the O.U.D.S. and he

26

had the most beautiful reading voice. So had Clifton. Then the fourth one was Guy Chapman who eventually became a Professor of History. Rather amusing, for what it's worth, for we all of us, except Clifton Gordon who died young, eventually got into Who's Who."

For most of the time, though, life was conducted along traditional public school lines.

"In those days life was considerably more strict. We weren't a permissive society in any way. On the other hand, if anything, we were over-regulated and there was a mass of small rules of this, that and the other; you didn't do this or you didn't do that. The result was the same – you were beaten. Beatings were common. I remember when Adrian and myself had to beat two small boys who were brothers. I'd never beaten anybody before, nor had Adrian. We were far more frightened than the two small boys: hardened little criminals who knew all the tricks of the trade! For instance, the further you bent over, the smaller the target you presented. However, we managed to beat them somehow. I don't think they were very much hurt. Later, of course, one got terribly expert. It was all very solemn, very formal, a regular sort of trial, but it was fair. The miscreant would be given every opportunity of explaining. If eventually he was told we couldn't take that excuse he was told to go down to the Old Hall and wait outside. We'd go down and he'd be told to take off his coat. You were beaten in a very gentlemanly but painful way, simply by bending over a certain table. The old Westminster tanning pull, as we called the cane, was really a fierce instrument, much longer and thicker than the ordinary one.

"When I was Head of the House I tried to cut it out as much as I could, but it was very difficult because it was the one recognised punishment – we never gave lines or anything, so that you knew what would happen if you offended. However I don't think Adrian was ever beaten. It was comparatively rare for half-boarders."   (L.E.T.)

Sport was considered a necessary but not paramount part of the curriculum and Boult, although he shot for the school at Bisley, had to wait until he went up to Oxford to row competitively. But there were chances in the holidays and, as he reported back to Tanner, fresh possibilities with the advent of motoring now he was older.

"April 17th, 1907. Abbey Manor, West Kirby. This morning I took the car out. They have been trying a new and cheap brand of petrol

Mr Ralph Tanner, Boult's housemaster at Westminster, taken by Adrian Boult c.1904. The view through the arch of Dean's Yard shows Broad Sanctuary as it was, before the construction of Central Hall, Westminster.

Photo Jane Whitton

L. to R.: A. C. Boult, D. M. Low and O. V. Thomas in Ashburnham Garden, Westminster School, 1908.   *Photo Jane Whitton*

Two musical Christmas cards sent from Boult to the Tanner family in 1908 and 1911. Both show original piano compositions by Adrian Boult.

Photo Jane Whitton

and she doesn't like it at all – in fact soon after starting it was only with great difficulty that I persuaded her to overtake a cab which was proceeding along Meols Drive – well, at a cab-like pace. After this, in an evil moment I decided to go and row on the lake . . . I started off in a small outrigger (I can't say I'm really *comfortable* in an outrigger yet!) and soon discovered that the prize idiots had given me two right oars, so I kept losing the left hand one when I was resting. The wind was strong and I had to row hard for twenty-five minutes to get back to the boat house."

CLUBS AND SOCIETIES.

OXFORD LADIES' MUSICAL SOCIETY.

Programme for performance on Friday, June 17 :—

Trio for Flute, Violin, and Viola in D major, Op. 25 . *Beethoven.*

Songs
- (a) Der Kreuzzug .
- (b) Die Forelle .
- (c) Der Tod und das Mädchen
- (d) Wohin? .

. *Schubert.*

Quartet (arranged from "Die Kunst der Fuge") for two Violins, Viola, and Violoncello—
- (a) Contrapunctus III
- (b) Contrapunctus IX

. *J. S. Bach.*

Songs
- (a) Mit Myrthen und Rosen
- (b) Der Nussbaum . .
- (c) Wanderer's Nachtlied .
- (d) Mandoline . . .

. *Schumann.*
Liszt. .
Debussy.

Quartet (arranged from "Die Kunst der Fuge") for two Violins, Viola, and Violoncello—
- (a) Contrapunctus XI .
- (b) Contrapunctus XV (unfinished)

. *J. S. Bach.*

Songs
- (a) Im Kahne . . . . . *Grieg.*
- (b) Ablösung . . . . . *Hollander.*
- (c) Die Lehre . . . . *Van der Stucken.*
- (d) Le cœur de ma mie . . . *Dalcroze.*

Singer—Dr. LIERHAMMER. *Flute*—Mr. BOWMAN. *Violins*—Miss M. VENABLES and Miss D. TYNDALE. *Viola*—Mr. PAUL DAVID. *'Cello*—Mr. O. H. GOTCH. *Accompanist*—Mr. A. C. BOULT.

Programme for a concert in 1910 with Boult as accompanist. Incredibly, this concert included the first known public performance of any of *The Art of Fugue.*

At the end of the Election (Summer) Term, 1908, Adrian Boult left Westminster to go to Christ Church, as planned, while Lawrence Tanner stayed on an extra year to become Head of Grant's, before going up to Pembroke College, Cambridge. For Boult, the intervening time was spent in Scotland (in the company of friends who came to stay), writing his own music, not always, it seems, to his complete satisfaction:

"7th Sept. 1908, Glencaird. Dear Lawrence. I am quite crackly this morning. It's raining, and I ought to be working at a wretched old Piano Trio or something – oh, why am I so lazy?

"I have learnt 10 Brahms songs with which to convert you to him. After that I *know* you will sing his praises.

"The Infant [Guy Chapman] *did so* enjoy being awakened every morning to be taken to the river before breakfast, especially if it was cold. He used to stand on the brink and cry loudly when I got him down there, and would only go in if I threatened to push him."

"Adrian was always painfully awake; bullying us to go bathing before breakfast or something awful!" (L.E.T.)

"I began fairly well at Oxford. I read History for my first year, but Hugh Allen was very much on top in those days and he was doing far too much. He was going to London to do the Bach Choir as well as his Oxford work, and so I had deputizing to do for him very soon after I got there. He was very kind to me and let me in on a great many things. Actually, he persuaded me to give up trying for the honours school and to take just a pass degree and a musical degree at the same time, so I was thoroughly in music by the end of my fourth year." (A.C.B.)

The Edwardian social life at Oxford was considerably more of a strain on the stamina than academic work.

"29th. Oct. 1908. Christchurch. I find that quite a lot of people neither drink nor smoke here, but the awful sociableness of the place nearly kills me although I love it. I think I have had two or three breakfasts alone in my rooms this term and not a single tea! My rooms (which are quite respectable, by the way – although the furniture is of the rather ancient and shabby splendour order, and consequently rather rickety) are in the most accessible place in College – consequently they are always full of people. This of course I enjoy hugely, but work is *rather* difficult, as you may imagine. Then the iniquitous system of fresher's having to call and call again until they find people in is rather a trial. I'm sure I've paid about thirty calls in consequence. H. I. P. Hallett alone is responsible for five!"

(A.C.B. to L.E.T.)

With the encouragement of Hugh Allen, then Professor of Music, the foundations of Boult's future were laid. He already knew Elgar, from the gatherings at Frank Schuster's house, but another friendship proved to be prophetic and significant for English music. At the end of 1909 Lawrence Tanner wrote telling him about a performance of Aristophanes' 'The Wasps' which he had been to in Cambridge. Boult's reply was disappointing but rather capped his friend's experience.

"3rd December 1909. Christchurch, Dear Lawrence, Thank you for your letter. Yes it was piggy not being able to see the Wasps. I *do* know a little of the music, though. Vaughan Williams brought it in to Allen's house one Sunday morning last term when I was there and he played, Allen sang tenor, and I bass – we had great fun and Allen and I sang *far* better than VW *played*, although it was his own stuff. Allen told him to go away and learn the piano!"

The Years in Birmingham

LYNDON JENKINS

'It was Sir Henry Wood who recommended me to Birmingham when he gave up the conductorship of the Birmingham Festival Choral Society in 1923', Sir Adrian told me. 'I was delighted to have a choir of my own to conduct, of course, and even more delighted when I was offered the City of Birmingham Symphony Orchestra some months later.'

The job required Sir Adrian to live in Birmingham. 'I found digs in a fine house in Church Road, Edgbaston, not far from what is now the Edgbaston Golf Club, very efficiently managed by a Mrs Groves as a private hotel', he said. 'I set up an office on the corner of Bennett's Hill and Colmore Row, and there I was helped by Harold Gray.' Gray's association with the CBSO was to prove a long and happy one: he relinquished his post as Assistant Conductor of the orchestra in 1979. 'Later on we moved down into the Bull Ring in the city centre.'

Although he had settled in Birmingham, Sir Adrian made sure that he kept in touch with the Metropolis. 'I used to catch the train from Snow Hill station on Friday mornings, after the Thursday evening concerts', he said. 'There was always somebody travelling that one knew, so the musical politics of Birmingham would echo down the breakfast car. In those days the journey took two hours to London – and the train was never late!'

The full orchestra of sixty played in the Town Hall on Thursdays and a smaller one of thirty-three players gave concerts on Sundays in the Futurist Cinema. The young Paul Beard, who was later to lead for Sir Adrian's BBC Symphony Orchestra, was the principal violin.

'The Futurist Cinema had no backstage facilities, you know, and I once found myself changing there in full view of the audience! There were fifty concerts in the winter season. In the summer the orchestra disappeared for the holiday months to play in pier bands at the seaside.

'When they came back I always dreaded the first week of the season because I had to set about teaching them to be an orchestra again. Indeed, I once broached this unsatisfactory state of affairs with my committee, but they were quite unperturbed: "Oh yes," they said, "you'll have to do that every season".'

Sir Adrian thought one answer to the problem might be to find work for the orchestra locally in those summer months. 'We were already visiting some of the Midlands public schools like Rugby and Oundle and I began to talk to municipalities such as Cheltenham to see whether they would take the whole orchestra for a few weeks each summer. But before we got very far my period at Birmingham came to an end; I believe such a scheme was implemented some years later, though.'

Mention of Cheltenham brought up the name of Gustav Holst, whose *Planets* suite has been a Boult speciality ever since he conducted the first performance of the work in 1918 before a private audience of the composer's friends. The hire of Queen's Hall and its Orchestra had been paid for by Balfour Gardiner. 'Since no orchestral parts of the work existed, they were copied out by teams of girls from St Paul's School, and as the parts were copied, each *Planet* was sent round for me to study.'

He reminded me that Holst had written *The Planets* because he wanted to, never thinking that he would ever have a chance to hear it performed. 'So you can imagine his excitement that Sunday morning in Queen's Hall. He was pacing up and down the stalls as I conducted and when I queried some detail with him he said 'I really don't know. I'm glad you're there as I have quite lost my head already'.

'Of course Granville Bantock was the hub of Birmingham's music at that time.' (He was Principal of the Birmingham School of Music.) 'I met him one day coming out of the Midland Institute and he said to me "Come and see what they have done to the Town Hall". Inside we found that in reorganising the interior they had made the balustrades of the lower gallery continue right across the platform so that it effectively cut the playing area in half. Bantock was *furious*. He went straight back to his office and wrote a letter of protest to the Lord Mayor, saying that if he did not have a reply within three hours he would send his letter to the *Birmingham Post*. He got his reply.'

Sir Adrian's six years in Birmingham were the only time in his life when he was able to choose all his own programmes. Where soloists were concerned, of course, the CBSO concentrated mainly on British artists, but the orchestra was visited by some of the great continental conductors, notably Bruno Walter and Ernest Ansermet. 'Though the orchestra was smaller than it is now, we managed to do some repertoire which was pretty new, such as Bartók's *Dance Suite* and Mahler's *Song of the Earth* and Fourth Symphony as well as many British works of course.'

Although he had signed a ten-year contract, during his sixth season the call came from the BBC to be their Director of Music and take charge of the new BBC Symphony Orchestra.

Since 1930, Sir Adrian has conducted in Birmingham on many occasions and even returned for a season as Principal Conductor in 1959-1960. Unfortunately, illness prevented him from appearing at the concert in October 1974, which would have marked the jubilee of his 1924 appointment. He last conducted the City of Birmingham Symphony Orchestra in Worcester Cathedral in September 1977, one of his last public appearances.

LYNDON JENKINS is a Birmingham-based music critic writing for the Birmingham Post, Classical Music and others. This is a revised version of an article which first appeared in the Birmingham Post.

Overleaf: Sir Adrian Boult during the recording of the 'Dream of Gerontius'.
Photo by courtesy of EMI Ltd.

Tribute

ERNEST HALL, OBE

I first saw Sir Adrian conduct a concert at the Sun Hall in Liverpool in which my father was a member of the orchestra. I became associated with him first at the Royal College of Music, and later when I was appointed Principal Trumpet and he Conductor of the BBC Symphony Orchestra. I had the honour of being chairman at his 60th Birthday Dinner which the orchestra gave at the Savoy Hotel, with Dr Vaughan Williams as Chief Guest. Sir Adrian's conducting was unpretentious and totally sincere; no showmanship and full of appreciation for members of the orchestra. I have said before that in my long experience as an orchestral player, and as one who has played under most famous conductors from Richter onwards, in my opinion Sir Adrian and Bruno Walter were the two most sincere conductors who ever stood on a rostrum.

Ernest Hall.

ERNEST HALL (b.1890) joined the London Symphony Orchestra in 1912, becoming its principal trumpet in 1924. He joined the BBC Symphony Orchestra as principal trumpet in 1930. He was also Professor of Trumpet at the Royal College of Music 1925-1970. He was awarded the OBE in 1962.

At Work With The Orchestra

Left: Sir Adrian Boult with André Previn.
Overleaf: Sir Adrian Boult

Photo by courtesy of EMI Ltd.
Photo by courtesy of EMI Ltd.

At Work With The Orchestra 1

BERNARD SHORE, CBE

Among the contemporary conductors of international fame, Adrian Boult represents Idealism. He is an idealist in his incessant striving after the most faithful approximation possible to the composer's mind. It is an essentially different attitude from that of the conductor whose principal aim is the finest possible playing and who, almost necessarily therefore, uses a composition as a vehicle for his own art rather than as a source of inspiration.

Adrian Boult's quiet stance on the rostrum, the economy of his gesture and his general stillness give a strong impression of restraint. His rigid self-control is no studied pose but the man himself. Disliking all forms of showmanship, he prefers to be an almost impersonal medium between the composer, orchestra and audience rather than the central character of a drama. His mind seems to brood over the score from a height, surveying all its essential features like the peaks of a mountain range seen from a certain distance. The proportions are thus truly discerned, with the greatest peaks duly towering above the rest. This amounts to saying that Boult is at his best in musical compositions that can be said to have architectural character, and is less at ease in the slighter music of fantasy and colour.

This 'idealistic' attitude quite frequently entails a departure from traditions – the traditions that have only too often been formed in the course of years by a succession of conductors who held personal success to be more important than loyalty to the scores in hand. There are musical compositions which, in whole or part, are regularly played in a way that – however regardless of the composer's intention – can be counted upon to tickle the public fancy, until in the long run a false tradition is firmly established.

But at rehearsals Boult will characteristically say: "No *crescendo*! If the composer had wanted one there he would have put one in". Or, again, when rehearsing some much-edited work of Bach: "Take out all those slurs! It is only one of those infernal editors again – there is no trace of anything of the sort in the original".

The *Figaro* overture is more often than not played at breakneck pace, and brings the house down by the virtuosity of the playing. But with Boult it is the crotchets that are *presto*, not the minims, though he, of course, beats two in a bar. As this is Mozart's own indication he prefers it to a more brilliant display.

On the subject of balance Boult is inexhaustible. He obtains his results by a very close study of the score and by persuading the players to use their intelligence to read between the lines of their parts with an alert ear for other instruments. If they are sitting too far from one another to hear adequately, then they must learn to know what is happening and adjust their tone accordingly. Balanced playing he regards as not solely the conductor's concern, but also one in which the players must take an active and intelligent interest. Faulty balance is at times the cause of an explosion. Thus:

"How on earth can you expect the clarinet to play his tune decently when you are lumbering along underneath like that? For goodness' sake, listen! Keep alive!" Mild enough words, no doubt; but there is plenty of meaning in the voice.

He attaches particular importance to the balance as judged by the broadcast effect, and looks upon the microphone as a valuable gauge. In his view, the balance, if right for the microphone, will certainly be right in the hall. On the other hand, what will do in the hall is not necessarily good enough for the microphone. He consequently makes full use of the BBC's Balance and Control Department, requiring of it confirmation of doubtful points in rehearsals for public concerts as well as studio performances.

Another characteristic of his rehearsals is his insistence upon rhythmic swing. Scarcely a rehearsal is without resort to this expression. Rhythmic swing he regards as the very life of musical performances, and nothing so much exasperates him as a wooden accent mechanically bumping on the first of the bar.

42

"No, no! It all sounds dead. Do swing the rhythm over from the end of each second bar to the third, and so on! Only be careful when the bar-groups alter in the 10th bar." This kind of thing also happens on the last note of a phrase, as in the opening of Mozart's G minor Symphony where the first violins go over to their B flat.

"Firsts, be careful! That B flat sounds the loudest note in the phrase. I want to hear it; but don't sit down on it so hard!" But although for ever insisting upon vital rhythm he does not fail to warn the players against self-conscious rhythm – the rhythm that is applied without being felt. All, in truth, that he wants is the style in which every chamber player is brought up.

Another aspect of style – the cultivation of the characteristic style proper to different composers or schools – forms an important study in his training of the orchestra. The differences are naturally subtle, but to the great breadth of a Brahms phrase he gives a certain character that is the very antithesis to what he requires in a similar phrase in Franck's symphony. He conceives the French schools as demanding an almost exaggerated attention to neatness and compactness of phrasing, with rhythmic figures generally as crisp as possible, while in Schumann and Brahms everything is required to be broad and spacious, while at the same time held well in control. But restraint is largely relinquished in Russian music, and here he stimulates violent changes of mood and colour.

The re-scoring of doubtful passages, especially in the classics, he utterly eschews; nonetheless, by great care in the subsidiary parts, he nearly always succeeds in establishing the essential line. If a wood-wind player had to complain that he has already been blowing "fit to burst" there is trouble for somebody. When, in the last resort, something really has to be done, it will be in the Beethoven, for instance, Weingartner's authority is sought. But this happens very rarely.

In Brahms practically no dynamic mark is allowed to be altered. Only, if the orchestra is large enough, the wood-wind is skilfully doubled. Results of remarkable clarity are obtained by complete but wary adherence to the score.

The dynamic marks of all composers prior to Rimsky-Korsakov and Elgar have naturally to be treated with a caution of which the more scrupulous moderns relieve the conductor. Brahms, for instance, impartially marks *forte* or *piano*, as the case may be, for all instruments, regardless of their difference of power. Boult, then, directs that the trumpet shall modify its *forte*, when it is necessary to match the horn; and so on, throughout the orchestra. Elgar, on the other hand, made allowances for this in his scrupulous markings, and Boult plays Elgar's scores quite literally.

Springing from the roots of his nature is Boult's humane consideration for the orchestra. It would be profoundly wrong to regard this as the sign of an easy-going character. It is really sound psychology, as well as the result of an appreciation of other people's feelings. He knows his players and can safely count upon them to give as intelligently as they can. Thus he avoids the orchestra's most dreaded bugbear – that vain repetition at rehearsals which breeds boredom, exasperation and ultimately inefficiency and staleness.

Boult's general rehearsal method is – in a symphony, for instance – to play, if possible, as far as the end of the exposition without stopping. Having an excellent memory, he can bear in mind the salient points calling for criticism; with the orchestra at rest he then discusses these points for a few moments. The passages criticized are now severally played but not, as a rule, the whole. Boult's rehearsals are a means to an end. Each one becomes a little more tense, but never does he aim at a peak until the performance proper. He holds physical freshness to be of more moment than any great achievement at rehearsal. He may require certain passages to be played with full power for the purpose of balance, but that power must be still greater "on the night".

"Horns, I don't want you to spoil your lip now, but give everything you've got tonight!" And again: "You see that the trombones don't support you at that point. You must carry the weight of the whole orchestra yourselves" – a characteristic sentence, in that it gives the players a clear reason for the demand made. Boult invites the orchestra to use its understanding in the performance of music. He does not look upon his players as mere cogs in a machine.

Boult is exceptionally still on the rostrum. He seems quite comfortable with about six inches of room on either side of him, and he never moves his feet. Every movement he makes is controlled; he relies almost entirely on the stick itself, which often follows the line of the phrase in a curve and rises just a fraction before the bar-line to make clear the swing. His left hand is used sparingly and never unnecessarily.

In *pianissimo* his stick scarcely moves at all, and it has then to be very carefully watched by those who are some distance away. For the really great moments his right hand will go back behind his body with an extra effort, but only at the top of a climax. That is his strength. By restraint and complete control over his own emotions and temperament and those of the orchestra he doubles his power when it is all wanted. And let no one think that he is too fond of the leash. Listen, for instance, to the *Flying Dutchman* overture under his direction. At those moments marked by Wagner for special fury, the winds scream with far more violence than is felt if the utmost is made of the top of every chromatic scale.

'Leonora No.3' comes naturally to mind as an illustration of Boult's methods at rehearsal, for nothing better shows his attitude as a faithful interpreter. It is the antithesis to the performances by conductors who so stamp their own personalities on the score that the effect is less Beethoven than a fantasy on a Beethoven theme. Boult seeks to impress Beethoven's mind upon the orchestra, and succeeds as few conductors do.

At rehearsal the first unison G has to be accurately balanced and corrected for faults of intonation in the wind, and the long *diminuendo* that follows over four bars has to be played until it really becomes a steady dwindling of tone. The *crescendo* in the next bar of the strings may go too far, or else the *diminuendo* begins too soon. "Up to the end of the third quaver strings only, or we shall never hear the bassoons!"

The semiquaver triplet passage between the flute and first violins goes a little awry. "Firsts, be careful that there is no gap after Mr X's F sharp! It's always a bit late, and I want it to fit perfectly, as one arpeggio between you – No! It's not together yet, firsts, but it is the early people who are right!"

In the bar before the big A flat major chord the trombones perhaps enter too loudly and so spoil the gradual *crescendo* already begun by the wood-wind. "Trombones, be careful to balance your tone with the wood-wind. Remember, they've only got up to *mf* on your entry. I want the tone built up steadily to the *fff*s."

After two or three shots at the A flat string passages for more brilliance, and then a good attack on the following chords, the little demi-semiquavers at the end of the bar are perhaps out of place. "Strings, they must be absolutely in place on the last semiquaver of the bar. Count four on that last beat!"

At the end of the *adagio* he probably finds it necessary to play it through all again, but then does not stop until the trumpet fanfare. Here, when he brings the orchestra to a standstill, he does not succeed in stopping the trumpet, who is, of course, off stage. "All right, Mr X! Oh, tell him, somebody. We must stop here – there is rather a lot that wants seeing to. First of all, it isn't alive, and you are not listening. Several wood-wind tunes were lost. Wind, those chords on the off-beats were all over the place. They must be on time, to fit the violin octaves.

"Strings, at the opening of the *allegro* you simply sat on those dotted minims, and then bumped your last crotchet of each phrase. Think of the tune in two-bar groups, with perhaps the slightest push at the beginning of each alternate bar. Basses, be careful too of your C's. Don't make them all alike!

"Then the great *crescendo* never really grew at all. You had used everything up before you got to the *ff*, which, incidentally, was a very poor affair. And I want still more power five bars later. Don't *crescendo* immediately you see it marked – remember how far you have to go, and make an absolutely steady piling-up to the crash at the *ff*. And at the *sempre ff*, five bars later, all you're worth!

"Violins and seconds, not too much *crescendo* on those accompanying triplet figures! They were altogether too heavy. And, all of you, please let me do as I like at the *pianissimo* bars later on. Some of you crashed in too soon at those repeated quavers. Those three silent beats are mine, and you will kindly not encroach on my private property. Strings, there was no attack at all on the scales leading up to the trumpet. I want a terrific attack after that quaver rest, and I make no pull-up whatever."

After one or two things have been put straight he starts again just before the fanfare, but bad articulation of the little rhythmic figure in the strings makes him stop and speak to the leader.

"Mr X, I want those rhythmic figures clearer and yet dead *pp*. Can you get it better for me?"

Mr X's reply is to the effect that some of the players are not ready with their bows on the string, and also it is better to use the point of the bow. All then goes well, perhaps, until the run-up of the flute at the return, when the strings are admonished for being too loud. The violin cadenza makes him mutter, "We'll see to that later." The *crescendo* at the end again is unsatisfactory, and he directs that the tone is not to be dropped at the place usually marked *mf*, since the trombones enter there and it is unneccessary. On the other hand, a slight drop to help the *crescendo* may be made four bars later, when the trombones stop. The *crescendo* is then piled up to *fff* (the one *f* can be ignored). This climax crowns the whole work, and must be made even more intense than the A flat chord in the introduction and the first *ff* in the *allegro*. "Last of all, don't play all the chords at the end alike. Make the last one the biggest!"

In tackling new works Boult will do his utmost to get the composers to be present, at least for one rehearsal, in spite of the fact that they frequently upset the timing and are apt to be difficult. But provided they know their own minds, all goes well. If he cannot, as in the case of *Wozzeck*, have the composer, he obtains, for fear of misreading the composer's directions, the presence of some authority like Herr Prerauer of Berlin, who first produced *Wozzeck*.

It has often been noticed that Boult not only knows the complicated scores of Schoenberg, Bartók, Berg and the like from beginning to end, but can also make them intelligible to his orchestra without any agitation or extra rehearsal. When foreign specialists come over to conduct them their knowledge is apparently no deeper; they have infinite difficulty in making themselves understood, even with a good interpreter, and invariably have to be helped out with longer or extra rehearsals. To say nothing of an exasperated orchestra into the bargain.

It is a feature of Boult's technique as a conductor, this quick assimilation of scores in every kind of idiom. He finds his way about quickly, and is able to take the orchestra with him straight to the root of the matter. He organizes both other people and himself, smoothly and without fuss or agitation; and although his repertory covers the whole realm of orchestral music, he conducts most of the well-known works from memory. It is significant that when Toscanini conducted the BBC Orchestra in 1935, in his rehearsals he scarcely touched Brahms' Fourth Symphony or the *Enigma Variations* – two of Boult's greatest interpretations. He was indeed able actually to cut down the allowance of rehearsal time – a tribute to Boult's orchestra training.

Being an Englishman, without any natural showmanship or the prima donna's temperament usually found in famous conductors, Boult may possibly never become a popular idol, but there are few conductors in the world who surpass him in the art of true interpretation.

BERNARD SHORE (b.1896) was principal viola in the BBC Symphony Orchestra. This article, which first appeared in 'The Orchestra Speaks', is reprinted by kind permission of the author.

At Work With The Orchestra 2

SIDONIE GOOSSENS, MBE

The mere mention of his name brings to my mind memories of my youth (and his youth too) and my early meetings with this lovable man who was to decide my future years with his orchestra, the BBC Symphony Orchestra. To me he was always patient and helpful, but to many musicians he was not always so: he had a temper which, fortunately for all of us, he very rarely showed, yet it was there nevertheless – a warning to many when his voice was raised loudly as if through a megaphone!

Dr Boult, as he was known in those days fifty years ago, chose every member of the orchestra he was forming for the BBC and I was thrilled and overjoyed when I received a telegram while abroad on holiday telling me that I had been appointed principal harpist, the position I have held ever since. He trained this orchestra of young musicians who came from all over the British Isles, and made it into an instrument that attracted many of the greatest conductors in the world. His technique was an example to many aspiring young conductors who came to our rehearsals with their miniature scores. He always encouraged any student who wanted to learn, and what better master could they have had?

Our wartime years were spent together based in Bristol and Bedford. Under his direction we gave concerts at many British and American Air Force camps, and it was at these American camps that we were given the most wonderful food. Our own wartime rations were very meagre, and it did one's heart good to see Sir Adrian really enjoying a good meal. We always felt that he did not eat enough. Always a tall man with a fine physique, he walked miles – and when not walking he was a familiar sight cycling up and down the well-known hills of Bristol with a bicycle, tall like himself, on which he carried a large basket fixed on the handle bars to hold his many scores.

I am one of the fortunate musicians who worked consistently under Sir Adrian's baton from 1930 until he retired from the BBC in 1950, and of course until very recently when he conducted our orchestra. Besides playing all the classics of the great masters of the 18th and 19th centuries, we played the works of Sir Edward Elgar in the presence of Sir Edward with whom I became a close friend, and Dr Vaughan Williams, who incidentally liked to study the technique of the harp by sitting near me at rehearsals. This became a joke with Sir Adrian who once told him impatiently to "Go back to Harpist's Corner" in a loud authoritative voice when V.W. was by the rostrum looking over Sir Adrian's shoulder and obviously irritating him.

Sir Adrian must have conducted more music in those twenty years than most conductors would play in a lifetime. Our repertoire was enormous, and we gave many first performances of new works. We gave a concert of contemporary music every month and many British composers were represented as well as other nationalities including Central Europeans. We were already playing music by Schoenberg, Webern and Berg, in the early 30's including the first performance in England of Berg's *Wozzeck* (a concert performance). Sir Adrian was tireless; his rehearsals were thorough but he never over-rehearsed any work, which made us more alert and "on our toes" at the concert itself.

Sir Adrian has always been the kindest and dearest friend, sympathetic in sad times and always helpful and appreciative of one's work. Although he does not appear in public any longer it is good sometimes to hear his rich voice calling over the phone and having a nice chat with him. I am deeply grateful to him for all his help over many years and for the great affection he has always shown me.

SIDONIE GOOSSENS, the harpist, is a member of the illustrious musical family which also produced the conductor and composer Sir Eugene Goossens and the oboist Leon. She has been principal harpist of the BBC Symphony Orchestra since its inception.

At Work With The Orchestra 3

MARIE WILSON, MBE

My first meeting with Adrian Boult was when I became a student at the Royal College of Music in January 1919. Although very young to be admitted to Senior College (I was just fifteen), I was fortunate enough to be placed in the 'First Orchestra', at that time conducted by Sir Charles Stanford. Not very long after I joined, he retired and Sir Adrian took over. He was a strict master and sometimes could be fierce (though not as much as Stanford). But I remember a rehearsal in the Concert Hall one day when I was sitting at the back of the violins. Suddenly a finger shot out. "You!" I looked round to see who was the object of his temper. "No; you! Out!" For once in my life I wasn't talking, but I still found myself outside the hall.

Things were rarely that disagreeable, of course. A little later he asked whether there was anybody who would be interested in playing in the orchestra he formed each year for the Petersfield Festival and I volunteered, playing in the Festival concerts in the Old Drill Hall for ten years. My clearest memories of those years, though, is of my first College concerto concert. The programme began with Smetana's *Vltava*. Usually I would have played in the orchestra for that but since I was to play the Brahms concerto immediately afterwards I was allowed to miss it, though I had to go back to my leader's seat for Beethoven's Seventh Symphony after the interval. He was a marvellous accompanist because he was not busy with the beat all the time. Instead he would be very still and quiet, really following the soloist, and at the end of a solo passage he waited, never taking up the beat until just the right moment.

While I was still a student at the Royal College I started to play in the Queen's Hall Orchestra, very much, of course, the domain of Sir Henry Wood. It was under his influence that women really started to be given a place in the orchestra as a direct result of the First World War, when so many of the men were taken out of the profession to the fighting. Then in 1929 the BBC Symphony Orchestra was formed from a nucleus of players from the Queen's Hall; I was offered the No.3 seat and it is from then that my friendship with Adrian really dates.

Then, as now, the orchestra's main concert took place on Wednesday nights and in the early days there was a wonderful atmosphere about them. We were all young, all committed. One would come out into Oxford Street in a bemused state, unable to talk, and we'd sit in the upstairs café at Appedrodt's Delicatessen (no longer in existence) still under the magical influence of those concerts. There were about twenty women (quite a large number for those days) and at one time it was suggested that we wear 'dinner jacket suits'. The majority of us, though not all, agreed to this idea. I remember that I had a black silk skirt and jacket, with a white chiffon pleated shirt with crystal cuff-links made by Sidonie Goossens' French dressmaker. Sidonie was – and still is – a marvellous player with a tremendously attractive personality.

In 1935 and 1936, before Paul Beard took over, I led the orchestra at the Proms. Then the war came. One Friday night Sir Henry Wood made a speech to the orchestra, something he never normally did, and the next day we moved to Bristol. The Blitz was terrible. People said that the Germans waited for the BBC to arrive before they started! I lived in a street just round the corner from the studios and all around me the houses were destroyed; even the house next door was burned down. We would record in the morning so that we could be safely home before the searchlights and the bombing began. Adrian, though, had a lovely house over Clifton Bridge and it was always a relief to go out there for tea, away from the city.

It was quieter when they transferred us to Bedford two and a half years later. We gave our concerts in the Corn Exchange and it was while I was there, in 1944, that three tragic things happened all in the same week. Sir Henry Wood died, so did Ida Kersey (a fine violinist who was the first person to play the Bax concerto) and my five-year-old daughter. It was then that Adrian became almost a father-confessor, sympathetically listening to my troubles on long walks through the woods and countryside of Bedfordshire.

I resigned from the BBC at that time and for two or three years resumed a career as a soloist but I have also been associated with Sir Adrian in two coronations. The first in 1937 and the second in 1953 when I had the honour of taking part as one of the violinists in a company of many distinguished musicians. At one time, when I used to lead a section of the BBC orchestra, I had been very concerned that I did not have enough authority to be the leader, that I would find it

Sir Adrian Boult.   *Photo by courtesy of EMI Ltd.*

difficult to impose the necessary discipline. 'Don't worry about that', he told me, 'the best discipline is example.'

Now it is his example that remains of greatest value (although there is no lack of authority, partly from the force of his character, partly from the breadth of his education), for there is no conductor who is more faithful to the score. Leslie Woodgate, one-time chorus-master at the BBC, once said that only the composer is a genius, the player is there only as an executive to present him. Adrian Boult presents the composer with a great and wise integrity which permeates his nature. He is not a showman and he has never been a particularly 'box-office' conductor, yet there is nobody who can do more justice to Brahms, Schubert or Elgar, for he sees beyond the beat and the bar line to the sense of phrase in a way impossible for most conductors. As soon as he stands on the box, he gives you a shape, not just a time signature. He always expects the best of an orchestra and will not stand for anything half-hearted. I remember a player once coming to him complaining that he did not like the piece we were working on. 'You might like it better', he retorted, stroking his moustache, 'if you could play it better.'

His extraordinary sympathy with a composer's intentions can have strange results. Years ago the BBC orchestra gave a serenade concert in the cloisters of Canterbury Cathedral. I was playing the solo part in Vaughan Williams' *The Lark Ascending*. I played the piece many times and am proud to remember that when I played it to him for his advice he remarked to a friend 'dear Marie, she plays more like a lark and less like a nightingale.' On the occasion of the Canterbury concert it was a fine summer evening, and as the sound of the music died away into the quiet dusk the birds in the rafters started to sing.

MARIE WILSON (b.1903) played with the BBC Symphony Orchestra from the start and has been a friend of Sir Adrian's for many years. She is at present a member of the London Philharmonic Orchestra.

At Work With The Orchestra 4

COLIN BRADBURY

Unlike Victorian children, conductors should be heard and not seen. They should speak to the audience through the orchestra and their conducting should be a private language which they share with the players. Every gesture designed to impress the audience is, in the end, a distraction, and, for the music and the musicians, a moment wasted.

Few conductors consistently attain this ideal. Rudolf Kempe was a fine example, as was Pierre Monteux, but among living conductors it is Sir Adrian whose musical integrity undoubtedly earns him the title of a 'musicians' conductor'.

The beat, especially at rehearsals, is terrifyingly vague on first acquaintance; one end of the enormous stick remains stationary, whilst the other swishes through a two-foot arc, always a little ahead of the players. There are none of those jerky stops and starts which look so tight and precise to the layman but are unpredictable and meaningless to the musician; the stick flows as the music flows – rhythmically. Rehearsals are never long, drawn-out affairs; everyone is expected to know his job, and energies are saved for the concert. The shape of the music comes from the point of the stick, and at those moments when an orchestral soloist must be free, but must have a framework in which to exercise his freedom, Sir Adrian stands supreme. To play for example, the closing bars of the slow movement of Elgar's First Symphony in a Boult performance is, for me, to experience the ideal relationship between a conductor and a player.

His well-known tetchiness occasionally shows itself, giving rise to such oft-quoted remarks as "What's the matter – don't you like it?" – "Only taxi drivers smoke at work" and to a player obviously not paying attention, "What have I just said?". One can hardly imagine a younger man, however distinguished, being allowed to play the schoolmaster, but no one seems to resent it from Sir Adrian. His straightforwardness and lack of guile make it very difficult to bear a grudge. The remarks just become part of the legend, together with his enormous appetite for stodgy foods, coupled with his refusal to drink alcohol, tea or coffee.

At the concert the orchestra can be sure of music's most vital ingredient, the pulse. Far more important then beating time, the setting of a pulse on which the music can ride is the core of the conductor's art, and without it the rest is empty show.

To play the Schubert C major symphony with Sir Adrian is to realise how little a conductor needs to do, and how few men can do it. There is no obstacle between Schubert and the audience.

COLIN BRADBURY, active both as a soloist and orchestral player, has worked with Sir Adrian as principal clarinet in the BBC Symphony Orchestra for a number of years.

At Work With The Orchestra 5

ALAN CUMBERLAND

"Mr Cumberland, could I see you for a moment?"asked Sir Adrian Boult after rehearsal. He waited for most of the orchestra to disappear then, as he pulled my shoulders back sharply into an upright position, said: "You will never reach my age if you continue poking your neck like that. And by the bye, let's have a few less bumps in the middle of the bar, always lean on the first beat". He taught me so much about orchestral timpani playing and music in general and it was most fortunate for me that he was President of the LPO and we worked frequently together.

I shall never forget my first professional engagement with Sir Adrian – a recording for the BBC of Vaughan Williams' Fourth Symphony in the Maida Vale studios. At the time, I was being considered for the principal timpani position in the LPO and was, to say the least, a little apprehensive. My nerves were such that if I placed a stick on the drum it would roll by itself! Apart from this symphony having a few awkward corners, I was a complete stranger and did not feel entirely at home. After about fifteen minutes, during a tricky chromatic passage with the cellos, Sir Adrian addressed me across the orchestra: "You can help us all there, Mr Cumberland". Those few words were enormously comforting at the time.

We played a good deal of Elgar with him and he knew exactly how the music should be interpreted – it seems strange when other conductors come along with their own, sometimes weird, ideas as to how Elgar's music should sound. Even when Boult knew a work intimately his modesty was such that there was always an open score on the desk at concerts, and he would turn the pages gently from time to time.

Just one feature of his extraordinarily economical technique was that he could achieve a magnificent *fortissimo* with a short, sharp flick of his baton – usually with his eyes closed – together, and more forcefully than some of his colleagues who thrash about wildly and pull faces. One marvellous moment is the climax towards the end of the slow movement of Elgar's Second Symphony where Sir Adrian would say "You people at the back can put the lid on it there!"

He firmly believed in punctuality as part of our training and was always on the rostrum at least five minutes before the rehearsal was due to begin, and on the stroke of two o'clock or whenever, the stick came down. One evening at the Fairfield Halls, Croydon, our orchestra was playing for the first item on the programme something which involved everyone except the timpanist and I was talking to David Ward in the Artists' Bar (over a glass of bitter lemon); he was the soloist in *Wotan's Farewell*. David said "I'll see you in a minute" and thinking he was going to freshen up, I stayed in the bar. One minute later the orchestral manager's voice echoed around the backstage area: "Timps you're on!". Sir Adrian had stayed on the podium and David had gone straight onto the stage. I should have known what was going to happen. The piece begins with a timpani roll and, creeping on in as dignified a manner as possible, with one eye on Sir Adrian, I was stretching for my sticks when the long baton came down. In the desperate effort to begin with him, I sent the whole case of sticks crashing to the floor. He looked over with a wry smile and wink as if to say "That'll teach you a lesson". It did.

ALAN CUMBERLAND is currently Principal timpanist of the London Philharmonic Orchestra. He is also Professor of Timpani at the Royal College of Music.

Overleaf: Sir Adrian Boult with Sir Arthur Bliss.   *Photo by courtesy of EMI Ltd.*

Tribute
SIR LENNOX BERKELEY, CBE

Adrian Boult has been all through his life a real friend to living composers, approaching their work with understanding and minute attention to detail. His power of drawing beautiful and meaningful playing from the orchestra, with very little movement on his part, is truly extraordinary. His life gives us much to be grateful for.

Lennox Berkeley.

SIR LENNOX BERKELEY (b.1903) is one of Britain's most illustrious living composers. His Violin Concerto has been recorded by Menuhin and Boult for EMI. He is at present President of The British Music Society.

Sir Adrian Boult: An Assessment of his Career.

JERROLD NORTHROP MOORE

Sir Adrian Boult is a symbol for our civilisation, for he is one of the increasingly rare individuals whose career gives a clear measure of what used to be thought of as human progress. Ninety years ago the virtuoso conductor – as we know him today and take him for granted – did not exist. Yet the world into which Adrian Boult was born still believed in heroes: so there were still lively visions of what lay in the future to be dared and won. To stand beside Sir Adrian for a moment now at the summit of his life may give us a glimpse of those far landscapes of his youth and of the path forward he made through our century – the path he turned into a highway.

The new Oxford undergraduate in the autumn of 1908 staggered the Dean of Christ Church by stating quite categorically his aim of becoming an orchestral conductor. Such an aim had no precedent in an Oxford education then. Conductors in England usually conducted as a result of occupying some more distinguished position in education or the church. Except for Henry Wood, there was no Englishman who could study, prepare, and conduct any work old or new in the short spaces of rehearsal time available to a high technical and musical standard. And almost no one seemed to think there should be.

In the autumn of 1909, after a year at Oxford, the 20-year-old Adrian Boult read a paper to the Oriana Society entitled 'Some notes on performances'. He laid down three precepts for an ideal performance:

observance of the composer's every wish; clarity through an emphasis on balance and structure; a final effect of music made utterly without effort. They were to be the guiding principles of his own career. Then he evaluated the conductors of 1909:

'The conductors of the present day may be divided into three schools: there are the men who beat time, like Dr. Richter; who guide the orchestra, like Mr. Safonoff; and who hypnotise the orchestra, like Mr. Nikisch.'

Arthur Nikisch (1855-1922) was Boult's god. Nikisch exercised a precise control of ensemble, dynamics, rubato, and phrasing which even today leaps out of the grooves of his primitive gramophone recordings. He did this by revolutionising the conductor's stick technique, making its pivot the fingers and wrist rather than the elbow. And Nikisch had started at the Leipzig Conservatory a class for conductors. After Oxford, Adrian Boult was determined to go to Leipzig and study in that class. By the time he arrived there in 1912, Nikisch had retired from teaching. But he still conducted the Gewandhaus Orchestra: young Boult obtained a card to attend Nikisch's rehearsals – and thereby to study the technique at first hand.

He would have gone on to Vienna, but an overstrained heart forced him home. Within a few months he was conducting his first professional concert: the date was 27th February 1914, the place the Public Hall at West Kirby (where his parents lived), the orchestra part of the Liverpool Philharmonic. The programme ranged from a Bach Brandenburg Concerto to one of the earliest performances of George Butterworth's *The Banks of Green Willow*. When the war came in August, Boult was declared unfit for service: he drilled recruits from the Lancashire mines, and organised a series of concerts to employ local musicians whom the war had deprived of their livelihood.

By the beginning of 1918 he was ready for London, but was London ready for him? It needed a testimonial from the Liverpool Philharmonic before the London Symphony Orchestra would allow itself to be conducted by one of such little-known abilities as young Mr Adrian Boult. They need not have worried. Boult conducted a series of four LSO concerts at the Queen's Hall in which standard classics of the repertoire were interspersed with a magisterial survey of English orchestral music – works by Parry, Elgar, Holst, Vaughan Williams, Butterworth and Bax were given in performances most of which had been carefully supervised by the composers. After the concert which included his *London Symphony*, Vaughan Williams wrote:

'May I say how much I admired your conducting – it is real **conducting** *– you get just what you want and* **know** *what you want and your players trust you because they know it also.'*

But an air raid that night had kept the audience so small that Boult altered one of his later programmes to include the *London Symphony* again. It was quite typical: fifteen years later, when an Edinburgh audience showed what he regarded as insufficient appreciation for Walton's Viola Concerto with Lionel Tertis as soloist, Boult turned round and told them that they should have it all over again – and they did.

Those LSO concerts made it clear that a new force had entered the orchestral scene in London. Later in 1918, when Holst was given the present of a rehearsal and performance of his as yet unperformed *Planets*, it was Adrian Boult who was chosen to master the complex score. A few months after that he premièred the Delius Violin Concerto with its dedicatee, Albert Sammons. After he conducted Elgar's Second Symphony for the first time in 1920, the composer wrote:

'With the sounds ringing in my ears I send a word of thanks for your splendid conducting of the Sym: – I am most grateful to you for your affectionate care of it and feel that my reputation in the future is safe in your hands.'

The Director of the Royal College of Music, Sir Hugh Allen, asked Boult to start a conducting class on the lines of Leipzig. It was the first such class ever formed in England, and Boult created its curriculum from out of his own experience. In January 1921 *The Music Student* devoted a long article to 'this new departure in British Musical Education'. From that first small class has come all the later formal training for conductors throughout Britian. Yet an academic life did not hold Adrian Boult's fulfilment, and in 1924 he added to his RCM duties conductorship of the Birmingham Festival Choral Society and the Birmingham City Orchestra. So his energies were deployed up to the time of his 40th birthday in 1929.

Then came an invitation to become Director of Music for the BBC. It carried direct responsibility for the entire national broadcasting policy for light and serious music. As Boult himself described it:

'The whole body of programmes must be so chosen and arranged as to implement the general programme policy of the BBC; in other words, the gigantic crossword-puzzle must not merely be solved – it must have a definite meaning when it is finished.'

The task needed imagination, energy, good humour and tactful patience with superiors whose musical knowledge was less, or was least.

All this Boult was ready to accept. But he made it a condition that he should also conduct regularly for the BBC and secured approval to found the BBC Symphony Orchestra. Looking back on this gigantic double job of conducting one of the nation's leading orchestras and directing the musical policy of its sole broadcasting authority, he says: 'I must have been mad to attempt them both'. Yet he filled both positions with great satisfaction on all sides for almost fifteen years.

In that double position Adrian Boult made his greatest contribution to music in this country. It meant that during all those formative years of broadcasting, the entire direction of the most influential musical broadcasting authority in the world was in the hands of that authority's chief orchestral conductor – a man whose family background, education and personality gave him both the perspective and the expert ability to serve the most unselfish of visions. It was a unique moment in the history of forming public knowledge and public taste.

He was able to share his vision – and the standards he achieved for it – with audiences, players and conductors everywhere. He was able to guide the commissioning of works from the best native composers beginning with Elgar, Vaughan Williams and Holst. He conducted British premières of such important continental works as Berg's *Wozzeck*. When he took his orchestra on tour to Vienna, he gave the Viennese première of Schoenberg's *Variations for Orchestra* op 31. His programmes covered an enormous range of modern European and American works – of first performances but also invaluable second, third and fourth performances; and he built the orchestra to such a standard that the BBC could invite Toscanini, Koussevitzky and Bruno Walter to share its rostrum. The result was, I think, to lay the real foundation of London's present position at the centre of the world's music-making. It is to Adrian Boult more than to any other man that we owe the truly fabulous wealth of our music now.

The years since his retirement from the BBC in 1950 are more familiar to us – Sir Adrian as chief conductor of the London Philharmonic Orchestra through years of vigorous provincial and European touring as the friend and counsellor of musicians everywhere, and finally as the *grand seigneur* of the brilliant musical scene he has done so much to create. Each of us will have his own treasured impressions of this most valued spirit. One recent moment is vivid in my memory. It is the sight of Sir Adrian on a night in June 1978 entering the orchestra pit at the Coliseum to conduct Elgar's ballet *The Sanguine Fan*. Immaculate in wing collar and dress coat sharply contrasting in the glow of the music-stand lamps, he moved slowly among the players toward the rostrum, while many in the audience rose to give the applause the warmth of their gratitude. It was not the applause of sensation, but of sustained celebration for one of the finest presences to grace our civilisation and inform it.

JERROLD NORTHROP MOORE is a leading authority on the music of Elgar and the history of the gramophone. This article is a revised version of one first published in the 'Gramophone' and is reprinted by kind permission of the publishers. He has edited the book 'Music and Friends', a collection of the letters written to Sir Adrian Boult, published in 1979.

Overleaf: Sir Adrian Boult recording the 'Dream of Gerontius'.

Photo by courtesy of EMI Ltd.

Boult as Accompanist

PROFESSOR DENIS MATTHEWS

The first time I played with Sir Adrian was in 1944, during the last stages of the Hitler war. There was a great demand for serious music in the forces and at two concerts organised by ENSA we performed the Beethoven 'Emperor' concerto, later repeating it at the Corn Exchange in Bedford, which was one of the BBC's wartime refuges. Playing with Sir Adrian and the BBC Symphony Orchestra meant a great deal to me, since between them they had contributed so much to my musical upbringing. In the early 1930s young music-lovers living out of London already regarded radio and records as indispensable life-lines to the world of orchestral music. In the summer months radio brought us the Proms and Sir Henry Wood. Sir Adrian often spoke of his great admiration for Sir Henry and in fact shared in the direction of the Proms when they transferred to the Albert Hall after the destruction of the much-loved Queen's Hall. But in the pre-war and off-Prom season it was to Sir Adrian – or Dr Boult – that we looked. He had been in charge of the BBC Symphony from its beginnings in 1930 and raised it to international stature in no time at all. We all listened to his dignified readings of the classics, the Beethoven and Brahms symphonies and the Schubert Great C major symphony. There was his special service to British composers, not only Holst, Elgar and Vaughan Williams but less well-known names like R. O. Morris, whose Symphony I heard him conduct in a Festival of British Music in 1934. There were the concert performances of Berg's *Wozzeck* and Busoni's *Doktor Faust.* When he took the Schoenberg *Variations* op 31 to Vienna in 1936 with the BBC he was in fact introducing the work to most of the audience. And such well-worn Romantic classics as Tchaikovsky No.5? He often spoke of his early studies with Nikisch and modestly wrote off his impressive Tchaikovsky as 'Nikisch and water!'

But to return to the wartime 'Emperor'. I found, as I always did, that Sir Adrian was the most considerate of colleagues in a concerto and in fact the reverse of those conductors who felt it their duty to give a young soloist a lesson in front of the orchestra. His attitude was of support without interference and he even thanked me for playing the pianissimos, which were Beethoven's anyway. He was, however, adamant over two details concerning the platform arrangements and I heartily concurred with both of them. He was one of the first who always directed concertos from the orchestra's side of the piano: the advantages are obvious, since the conductor has far closer contact with the inner voices of the score and is neither obstructed by the lid nor deafened by the soloist. He also insisted on the separation of first and second violins to his left and right, underlining an antiphony that is implied in so many scores from Mozart to Elgar. We often discussed such matters in after-concert chats and I was always amazed that Sir Adrian should find time to write to me appreciatively when I held forth on various musical topics, such as the Beethoven quartets, in broadcast talks.

During the post-war years I played many concertos with Sir Adrian and always with pleasure: Mozart, Beethoven, Schumann, Rawsthorne, Ireland. When we went to Frankfurt together for a concert that included Beethoven's C major Concerto and Vaughan Williams' Fifth Symphony the players were impressed with his ability to transmit a new work to them and also with his knowledge of German. The press praised him and called him an English 'gentleman' no doubt because of his quiet outward manner. I often sensed that there might be a sleeping volcano beneath but only rarely saw it flare into life – over injustices to others, as it happened, such as when I had been misinformed about a rehearsal time. In more recent years I have enjoyed his conducting of the great works of the repertory more and more. I sent him a telegram of thanks after a broadcast of Brahms' Fourth Symphony and needless to say that I had a most courteous reply. I know too that orchestras have welcomed his wisdom and authority as an antidote to the superficial glitter of much of our age.

DENIS MATTHEWS (b.1919) often appeared as a soloist with Sir Adrian. He is currently Professor of Music at the University of Newcastle-upon-Tyne and is well-known both as broadcaster and concert pianist.

Overleaf: Sir Adrian Boult with Christopher Bishop.

Photo by courtesy of EMI Ltd.

In the Recording Studio

CHRISTOPHER BISHOP

When Sir Adrian was about seven years old, a portly musical friend presumed to help him by correcting one of his early compositions. This did not go down well, and the boy was found in a furious temper, referring to the friend as 'a sausagy dumpling that alters one's things'. I am glad I did not know that story when I first came to record Sir Adrian, in 1966. I was over-awed enough at the prospect, and if his reactions to 'alterations' had been so violent at the age of seven, what might they have been at seventy-seven? It is in the nature of a recording producer's job to 'alter one's things'!

In fact, I knew very little of Sir Adrian as a man, though naturally I knew his back view well from the concert hall. I had seen him, looking impossibly remote and tall, ever since I first started going to concerts, and there was little to tell how this rather forbidding man would react to being produced by someone half his age. But I need not have worried. Sir Adrian was kindness itself, and fortunately the work to be recorded was *The Music Makers*. Now, I adore Elgar's music, and what could be more exciting to an Elgarian than to work with someone who knew him, and his circle of friends? An additional helpful factor was that Janet Baker was the soloist, and nothing ever goes wrong with her around. The one mishap which I remember was that I got my musical knights confused, and called out over the intercom, "Ready thank you, Sir Malcolm". But Sir Adrian's kindness passed even that test – he merely chewed his moustache a bit, but the LPO enjoyed themselves.

We soon established a very happy working relationship; partly because we have very similar tastes in music, and because Sir Adrian works in what is, for me, the ideal way. He will rehearse, while we get a basic balance in the control-room. He will then record a fairly long section, and come in to listen. We discuss any musical problems, and any faults of balance, and he will then return and make his corrections. Occasionally he will ask Christopher Parker (who balances most of his records) to help him to achieve the balance he wants, but normally he will get the balance right in the studio. If an instrument cannot be heard clearly, he will ask the rest of the orchestra to play quieter. This may seem an obvious thing to do, but it is astonishing how many conductors either ask the balance engineer to 'bring the instrument out', or ask the musician to play louder, with the result that everyone is trying to out-play everyone else, and a musical balance becomes impossible. Sir Adrian is a great stickler for the observation of expression marks, and his scores are completely unmarked, so that he can see only what the composer wrote.

When everything is to his satisfaction, and mine, Sir Adrian will give a performance of the agreed section, and then he rings me on the intercom and says "Well – what about that?" Here I have to decide if another complete take is necessary, or if it is only a question of a few 'patches' to correct accidents which could not bear repeated listening. It is a considerable responsibility, because generally Sir Adrian does not listen again to that section (until, perhaps, the 'break'), and so leaves the decision to me.

It is a point of honour with Sir Adrian to do his recording in as few takes as possible. He knows that an orchestra's concentration and enthusiasm are going to flag if they are asked to keep on repeating a movement. He always apologises to us for any 'patches' we have to do. In an article in *The Gramophone Jubilee Book* he said: "I still feel each time I am asked to do a 'patch', to be superimposed on my original performance, that I am letting the side down, for I ought to be able to do the thing in one. Surely we should be able to treat our recording friends exactly as we treat audiences in the concert room?" If only all conductors and artists felt the same!

When I first arrived at EMI in 1964 Sir Adrian was being rather sparsely used, but I am glad to say that things have changed very much since then. As I look at the list of the 43 records I have made with him, to date, it is interesting to note that between 1965 and 1970 all were of Vaughan Williams and Elgar. It was in August 1970, when we were recording the *Enigma Variations* and *Job* with the LSO that we found that we had two spare sessions, because Sir Adrian and the orchestra had worked so efficiently. Here was a chance to start on something different, and I suggested a Brahms symphony. He decided that No. 3 was his favourite at the moment, and that recording was so successful commercially that I was allowed to complete the set of four. One might well ask why I started the Brahms symphonies in this rather hole-in-the-corner way. I am afraid there is a tendency to pigeon-hole conductors and Sir Adrian had been very busy doing the complete Vaughan Williams, and, of course *The Kingdom*, which we knew he would do with more authority than anyone. However, having 'served his time' in English music, I felt it was time that he put on record his magnificent Brahms and his famous Schubert Great C major. Having tasted blood (and most gratifying sales) we embarked on the Wagner series, and have just finished the fourth volume.

Paul Tortelier recording the Elgar Cello Concerto with Sir Adrian Boult and the LPO.   *Photo by courtesy of EMI Ltd.*

L. to R.: Dame Janet Baker, Sir Adrian Boult, Christopher Parker, Christopher
Bishop.   *Photo by courtesy of EMI Ltd.*

Sir Adrian Boult at a playback session with Recording Producer Christopher
Bishop and Balance Engineer Christopher Parker at EMI's Abbey Road
Studios.   *Photo by courtesy of EMI Ltd.*

Most critics and correspondents were delighted that we were not only recording British music but others felt that while many other conductors could do Brahms and Wagner, only Sir Adrian could do true justice to the British giants. The record companies can never win, of course, but I feel that the records we are making now are more representative of Sir Adrian's versatile genius than in the days when he was kept strictly to English music. I do not, of course, forget Lyrita's excellent work in that field.

The fact that he will be recording a rare Tchaikovsky work for us in April does not alter the fact that he has recently completed Elgar's *The Apostles*. This was a great undertaking, and one for which Elgarians have been shouting ever since *The Kingdom* was recorded. That was issued in time for Sir Adrian's 80th birthday, and I had hoped to issue *The Apostles* in time for his 85th (on April 8th) but, alas, the economic crisis intervened, and it will have to be postponed until the autumn. Suffice to say that it is all safely 'in the can', and is a glorious performance, and a worthy successor to *The Kingdom*.

And what of the future? There is more to come of Elgar, Vaughan Williams and Holst (*A Choral Symphony*), and my diary is filled with 'ACB' dates for the rest of the year. I know that his loyal gramophone public will be glad to know that though his concert appearances will be rather fewer, he hopes to continue making records. In 1966 he made only two records for us, in 1973 he made eight, and this year he has already made three. Not bad at 85! Sometimes I find myself forgetting he is so venerable – he certainly doesn't look it. He has excellent hearing, with still the finest ear for balance in the business. He doesn't wear glasses, even to read a manuscript score. He has a hearty appetite, and seems immune even to canteen food. He, also, sometimes forgets the disparity in our ages, and once asked me, as we crossed a street in Holborn if I remembered the crossing-sweeper who used to work there.

Sir Adrian's stern aspect gives the lie to his extremely kind and generous personality, and to me the warmth of his friendship, and that of Lady Boult, came as an unexpected bonus to the purely musical pleasure of working with him. But above all, what makes his performances so great is the strong sense of the architecture of his music which he manages to show. The 'sweep' of the music is what makes it so exciting. He never chops the phrases about, and this is evident in his technique of recording, which I have described. If I had to choose one record to show this it would be the first movement of the

Third Brandenburg Concerto from his recent set, where it sounds as if the movement is a huge up-beat to the last statement of the theme. That skill is what makes Sir Adrian Boult a great conductor.

★   ★   ★

I wrote the above tribute in the *Gramophone* in 1974, for Sir Adrian's 85th birthday. I have left it unaltered, as I wished to retain the present tense, rather than making it retrospective. In 1974 there were still a lot of records to come, among them the Wesendonk Songs with Janet Baker, *The Dream of Gerontius*, the two Elgar Symphonies, the Beethoven *Pastoral*, the Brahms Serenades and *The Planets*.

The last record Sir Adrian made was, characteristically, of little-known works by Parry – two of them first recordings. It was also to be my last production for EMI, as shortly afterwards I was offered the post of General Manager of the Philharmonia Orchestra. Needless to say, my decision to leave EMI was not uninfluenced by Sir Adrian's wish to stop recording, at least for a time. I consulted him about the move, and he was most positive in his advice that I should move on to fresh woods. But I have a great hope that one day he may feel inclined to return to the studio, and that I shall be able to produce for him again. We made sixty records together between 1966 and 1978, and every one was a great joy to make.

But even if my wish does not come true, those records still exist – hardly any have been deleted – and I consider myself very privileged to have been able to help in preserving Sir Adrian's great interpretations.

CHRISTOPHER BISHOP was a senior producer at EMI records and produced many of Sir Adrian Boult's recordings over a number of years. He is at present General Manager of the Philharmonia Orchestra. This article is a revised version of one which first appeared in the 'Gramophone' and is reprinted by kind permission of the publishers.

The Boult Example

RICHARD HICKOX

Sir Adrian always has time. He never seems rushed or flustered, and has always found time for the little things and for caring about people and players. For example, I did a radio programme some time ago and suddenly a letter came through the post saying how much he had enjoyed it; but he doesn't know me well – I've only met him once or twice – he's just prepared to take the time to make people feel that they matter to him. A conductor must try and do that because otherwise the players can feel used, and I don't think that is enough.

His technique, of course, is so interesting. He is quite right that the point of the stick is what matters, and you can control everything from the wrist with the point of the stick; the loudest moment, the softest moment, the most exact cue can be given with the tiniest flick, conveying everything that is needed, yet very few people would have the confidence not to give more gestures than that and I do admire that greatly. I have had consultation lessons with a number of conductors, including Sir Adrian, and conducting is a desperately hard subject to teach, but I feel the fault of his teaching is that he wants everybody to conduct in the way he does and it is just not possible to get people to copy him exactly. I would find it very difficult. I feel I want to put more of myself, more of my body if you like, into the music, and I suspect that, though it is still to be applauded and revered, his is a school that has passed.

His other trademark, of course, is his insistence on balancing and arranging the orchestra in the old traditional way. I must say that I am becoming more attracted to that. The argument has always been that for ensemble it is much better to have the fiddles close together. If you have the second fiddles on the right of the platform they are actually speaking away from the audience, whereas the first fiddles are speaking out. But in a lot of music where you have antiphonal passages between the first and second violins, the old arrangement is certainly eminently sensible, and I like the feeling that the bass is in the middle of the orchestra. However, though it has a lot to say for it, because they often have so much unison passage work, it is a much

Sir Adrian Boult with Josef Suk recording the Beethoven Violin Concerto.
Photo by courtesy of EMI Ltd.

safer arrangement to have the fiddles together. An ensemble can be much tighter when they are all in one section, and I think that the players prefer to be next to one another. But as with Baroque music, which he has continued to do in the tradition in which he was brought up, I suspect that while he is not willing to change the manner in which he does things because he is convinced about that way, he is glad to see the good in progress.

I do admire very much the fact that he is interested in all music and not just corners of it; and he lets the music ebb and flow beautifully. He keeps a tight rein but allows the rubato to be perfectly natural. I have certainly learnt from that and I have listened to his recordings and performances avidly.

Our particular common ground is English music and this takes me back to what I was saying about having time. Originally I wrote to him out of the blue, thinking that he might possibly have heard something that I had done; but he certainly had never met me, yet he was prepared to give up as much time as I asked. If I want to go through a score with him or if I am worried about points of stick technique he is always prepared to help. He is invaluable for the fact that he has had from the composer's lips instructions in nearly every instance. Tempo markings are often wildly inaccurate when written down by composers, but he knows that Vaughan Williams meant so-and-so because Vaughan Williams told him so, and Boult probably gave the first performance anyway. One really does go back two or three generations in history talking to him.

RICHARD HICKOX is Director of Music at St Margaret's, Westminster and Chorus-Master of the London Symphony Chorus, as well as being Principal Conductor of the City of London Sinfonia. He has worked with most of the leading British orchestras and has made several records of Baroque and British music.

Discography

NIGEL SIMEONE

This discography is as complete as possible. The record numbers used are those of the original issues and any subsequent reissue number has been omitted. The following is a list of abbreviations.

BBCC	BBC Chorus
BBCSO	BBC Symphony Orchestra
BrSO	British Symphony Orchestra
BroSO	Bromley Symphony Orchestra
CorC&O	Coronation Chorus and Orchestra
LCS	London Choral Society
Light SO	Light Symphony Orchestra
LPC	London Philharmonic Choir
LPO	London Philharmonic Orchestra
LSC	London Symphony Chorus
LSO	London Symphony Orchestra
MFO	Menuhin Festival Orchestra
NPO	New Philharmonia Orchestra
PCO	Paris Conservatoire Orchestra
PHI	Philomusica
PO	Philharmonia Orchestra
PPO	Philharmonic Promenade Orchestra
RPO	Royal Philharmonic Orchestra
SNO	Scottish National Orchestra
VOO	Vienna Opera Orchestra
VPO	Vienna Philharmonic Orchestra

ALFORD
Colonel Bogey	LPO	ST 750	(10/68)

ARNOLD
English Dances 1-8	LPO	LW 5166	(6/55)

AUBER
Masaniello: overture	BBCSO	DB 2364	(7/35)

J. S. BACH
Brandenburg Concertos 1-6	LPO	SLS 866	(12/67)
Concerto in C BWV 1061	A. Schnabel, K.-U. Schnabel		
	LSO	DB 3401-43	(3/37)
Mass in B minor: Qui Sedes and	Ferrier		
Agnus Dei	LPO	LXT 5382	(2/53)
St John Passion: All is fulfilled	Ferrier		
	LPO	LXT 5382	(2/53)
St Matthew Passion: Grief for sin	Ferrier		
	LPO	LXT 5382	(2/53)
Suite No. 3 BWV 1068	BBCSO	DB 1963-65	(2/34)
Violin Sonata No. 6 BWV 1019			
Prelude *arr. Pick-Mangianalli*	BBCSO	DB 1963-65	(2/34)
Fantasia and Fugue in C minor			
arr. Elgar	LPO	ASD 2970	(3/74)
The Wise Virgins *arr. Walton*	LPO	LXT 5028	(4/55)

BARSUKOV
Piano Concerto No. 2	Barsukov		
	NPO	SDBR 6167	(3/67)

BARTÓK
Divertimento	PPO	NCL 16011	(7/57)
Music for Strings, Perc. and Celeste	PPO	NCL 16011	(7/57)

BAX
The Garden of Fand	LPO	SRCS 62	(10/72)
Mediterranean	LPO	SRCS 62	(10/72)
Northern Ballad No. 1	LPO	SRCS 62	(10/72)
November Woods	LPO	SRCS 37	(10/68)
Tintagel	LPO	LXT 5015	(4/55)
	LPO	SRCS 62	(10/72)

BEETHOVEN
Coriolan: overture	BBCSO	DB 2101	(6/34)
	PPO	XRC 6001	(4/62)
	NPO	ASD 2667	(3/71)
Egmont: overture	BBCSO	DB 1925	(9/33)
	PPO	XRC 6004	(7/59)
Fidelio: overture	PPO	XRC 6003	(4/62)
Leonora No. 3: overture	PPO	XRC 6002	(4/62)
Piano Concerto No. 3	Solomon		
	BBCSO	DB 6196-99	(4/42)
Romance No. 2 in F	Bress		
	LPO	ST 730	(7/68)

The Ruins of Athens: overture and Turkish March	PO	7ER 5129	(4/59)
Symphony No. 3	PPO	XRC 6001	(4/62)
Symphony No. 5	PPO	XRC 6002	(6/59)
Symphony No. 6	PPO	XRC 6003	(6/59)
	LPO	ASD 3456	(4/78)
Symphony No. 7	PPO	XRC 6004	(10/62)
Symphony No. 8	BBCSO	DB 1764-66	(11/32)
Violin Concerto	Ricci		
	LPO	LXT 2750	(1/53)
	Suk		
	NPO	ASD 2667	(3/71)

BERKELEY

Violin Concerto	Menuhin		
	MFO	ASD 2759	(2/72)

BERLIOZ

Beatrice and Benedict: overture	PPO	CCL 30160	(5/60)
Benvenuto Cellini: overture	PPO	CCL 30159	(5/60)
Carnival Romain: overture	BBCSO	DB 2078	(11/33)
	PPO	CCL 30160	(5/60)
Le Corsaire: overture	PPO	CCL 30159	(5/60)
Les Francs Juges: overture	BBCSO	DB 3131-32	(7/37)
	PPO	CCL 30159	(5/60)
Rob Roy: overture	PPO	CCL 30160	(5/60)
Le Roi Lear: overture	BBCSO	DB 3093-94	(4/37)
	PPO	CCL 30160	(5/60)
Waverley: overture	PPO	CCL 30159	(5/60)

BLISS

Music for Strings	BBCSO	DB 3257-59	(10/37)
	LPO	ASD 3020	(12/74)
Rout	Power		
	BrSO	D 574	(8/26)

BORODIN

Prince Igor: Polovtsian March	BBCSO	DB 3049	(4/37)

BRAHMS

Academic Festival Overture	LPO	DB 9670/71	(11/51)
	PPO	NCL 16001	(8/56)
	LPO	ST 730	(7/68)
	LPO	ASD 2901	(6/73)
Alto Rhapsody	Sinclair,		
	PPO	NCL 16002	(5/58)
	Baker, LPC,		
	LPO	ASD 2746	(12/71)
Hungarian Dances 17 and 18	LPO	DB 9670	(11/51)
Hungarian Dances 19, 20 and 21	BBCSO	DB 3814	(7/39)
Piano Concerto No. 1	Backhaus		
	BBCSO	DB 1839-43	(3/33)

Piano Concerto No. 2	Schnabel		
	BBCSO	DB 2696-2701	(1/36)
	Kentner		
	PO	ALP 1704	(6/59)
Serenade No. 1	LPO	SLS 5137	(2/79)
Serenade No. 2	LPO	SLS 5137	(2/79)
Symphony No. 1	PPO	NCL 16000	(6/56)
	LPO	ASD 2871	(4/73)
Symphony No. 2	PPO	NCL 16001	(8/56)
	LPO	ASD 2746	(12/71)
Symphony No. 3	PPO	NCL 16002	(3/57)
	LSO	ASD 2660	(2/71)
Symphony No. 4	PPO	NCL 16003	(7/56)
	LPO	ASD 2901	(6/73)
Tragic Overture	BBCSO	DB 1803-04	(4/33)
	PPO	NCL 16004	(5/58)
	LSO	ASD 2660	(2/71)
Variations on a theme by Haydn	PPO	NCL 16003	(7/56)
	LPO	SLS 5137	(2/79)

BRIAN

Gothic Symphony — BBCSO, etc. LB 2601 (private recording)

BRIDGE

Cherry Ripe	LPO	SRCS 73	(4/78)
Lament for Strings	LPO	SRCS 73	(4/78)
Sally in Our Alley	LPO	SRCS 73	(4/78)
Sir Roger de Coverley	LPO	SRCS 73	(4/78)
Suite for String Orchestra	LPO	SRCS 73	(4/78)

BRITTEN

Four Sea Interludes and Passacaglia from 'Peter Grimes'	LPO	GSGC 14059	(5/66)

BRUCH

Kol Nidrei	Bunting		
	LPO	ST 698	(5/68)
Scottish Fantasia	Rabin		
	PO	33CX 1538	(6/58)
	Campoli		
	LPO	LXT 5453	(9/59)
Violin Concerto No. 1	Elman		
	LPO	LXT 5222	(10/56)
	Menuhin		
	LSO	ASD 2852	(4/73)
Violin Concerto No. 2	Menuhin		
	LSO	ASD 2852	(4/73)

BUTTERWORTH

The Banks of Green Willow	LPO	LXT 5015	(4/55)
	LPO	SRCS 69	(1/76)
Two English Idylls	LPO	SRCS 69	(1/76)

A Shropshire Lad	BrSO	D 520	(3/26)
	Hallé	C 3287	(6/42)
	LPO	LW 5175	(4/55)
	LPO	SRCS 69	(1/76)

CHAUSSON

| Poème | Menuhin | | |
| | LPO | DB 9759-60 | (6/52) |

CHOPIN

Piano Concerto No. 1 (Balakirev	Gulda		
orchestration)	LPO	LXT 2925	(7/54)
Funeral March arr. Elgar	BBCSO	DB 1722	(11/32)
	LPO	ASD 3050	(2/75)

CLARKE

| Trumpet Voluntary | LPO | ST 698 | (5/68) |

COATES

The Dambusters: march	LPO	ST 750	(10/68)
	LPO	SRCS 71	(4/78)
From Meadow to Mayfair: In the			
Country and Evening in Town	NPO	SRCS 107	(2/80)
The Merrymakers: overture	NPO	SRCS 107	(2/80)
Summer Days	NPO	SRCS 107	(2/80)
The Three Bears	NPO	SRCS 107	(2/80)
The Three Elizabeths			
'Queen Elizabeth': march	NPO	SRCS 107	(2/80)

DELIBES

Coppelia: suite	PPO	NLC 16009	(5/56)
Sylvia: suite	PPO	NLC 16009	(5/56)
Naila: waltz arr. Minkus	PPO	NLC 16009	(5/56)

DOHNÁNYI

Piano Concerto No. 2	Dohnányi		
	RPO	ALP 1514	(10/57)
Variations on a Nursery Theme	Katchen		
	LPO	LXT 2862	(9/64)
	Dohnányi		
	RPO	ALP 1514	(10/57)
	Katchen		
	LPO	SXL 2176	(7/60)

DVOŘÁK

| Cello Concerto | Rostropovitch | | |
| | RPO | ASD 358 | (7/58) |

ELGAR

The Apostles	Armstrong, Watts, Tear, Carol		
	Case, Luxon, Grant, LPC, LPO		
		SLS 976	(11/74)
	(includes talk by Sir Adrian Boult)		
Bavarian Dances 1-3	LPO	LW 5174	(7/55)
	LPO	ASD 2356	(3/68)

Caractacus: march	LPO	ASD 3050	(2/75)
Carillon	LPO	ASD 3050	(2/75)
Cello Concerto	Casals		
	BBCSO	DB 6338-41	(11/46)
	Tortelier		
	LPO	ASD 2906	(8/73)
Chanson de Matin	LPO	LW 5174	(7/55)
	LPO	ASD 2356	(3/68)
Chanson de Nuit	LPO	LX 5174	(7/55)
	LPO	ASD 2336	(3/68)
Cockaigne	LPO	ASD 2822	(9/72)
Dream Children 1 and 2	LPO	ALP 1379	(10/56)
	LPO	ASD 3050	(2/75)
The Dream of Gerontius	Watts, Gedda, Lloyd, LPC etc.		
	NPO	SLS 987	(5/76)
The Dream of Gerontius: prelude	BBCSO	DB 2194	(6/34)
Elegy	LPO	ASD 3050	(2/75)
Empire March	LPO	ASD 3388	(9/77)
Falstaff	LPO	DB 9603-06	(5/51)
	PPO	NCT 17003	(6/57)
	LPO	ASD 2970	(3/74)
Froissart	LPO	ALP 1379	(10/56)
	LPO	ASD 2822	(9/72)
Grania and Diarmid: suite	LPO	ASD 3050	(2/75)
Imperial March	BBCSO	DB 3163	(5/37)
	LPO	ASD 3388	(9/77)
In the South	LPO	ALP 1359	(6/56)
	LPO	ASD 2822	(9/72)
Introduction and Allegro	BBCSO	DB 3198-99	(7/37)
	LPO	ALP 1153	(7/54)
	LPO	ASD 2906	(8/73)
The Kingdom	Price, Minton, Young, Shirley-Quirk, LPC, LPO		
		SLS 939	(4/69)
The Light of Life: Meditation	LPO	ASD 3050	(2/75)
The Music Makers	Baker, LPC		
	LPO	ASD 2311	(5/67)
Nursery Suite	LPO	ALP 1359	(6/56)
Polonia	LPO	ASD 3050	(2/75)
Pomp and Circumstance Marches 1-5	LPO	ALP 1379	(10/56)
	LPO	ASD 3388	(4/77)
No. 3 only	LPO	DB 21588	(9/53)
The Sanguine Fan	LPO	ASD 2970	(3/74)
Serenade for Strings	BroSO	P 142 L	(8/64)
	LPO	ASD 2906	(8/73)
Symphony No. 1	LPO	ALP 105	(6/53)
	LPO	SRCS 39	(4/68)
	LPO	ASD 3330	(4/77)

Symphony No. 2	BBCSO	DB 6190-95	(1/45)
	PPO	NCL 16018	(7/57)
	SNO	SLLP 1021	(2/64)
	LPO	SRCS 40	(4/68)
	LPO	ASD 3266	(10/76)
Variations on an original theme ('Enigma Variations')	BBCSO	DB 2800-02	(5/36)
	LPO	ALP 1153	(7/54)
	LPO	ASD 2750	(11/71)
Violin Concerto	Campoli		
	LPO	LXT 5014	(4/55)
	Menuhin		
	NPO	ASD 2259	(4/66)
	Haendel		
	LPO	ASD 3598	(11/78)
Wand of Youth: Suite No. 1	LPO	ALP 1153	(7/54)
	LPO	ASD 2356	(3/68)
Wand of Youth: Suite No. 2	LPO	ASD 2356	(3/68)
FALLA			
El Amor Brujo: Ritual Fire Dance	LPO	ST 698	(5/68)
FINZI			
The Fall of the Leaf	LPO	SRCS 84	(4/78)
Introit	Friend		
	LPO	SRCS 84	(4/78)
Nocturne	LPO	SRCS 84	(4/78)
Prelude for String Orchestra	LPO	SRCS 84	(4/78)
Romance for String Orchestra	LPO	SRCS 84	(4/78)
A Severn Rhapsody	LPO	SRCS 84	(4/78)
FRANCK			
Symphonic Variations	Curzon		
	LPO	SXL 2173	(2/60)
Symphony in D minor	LPO	GL 25004	(10/76)
GERSHWIN			
Cuban Overture	LPO	ST 698	(5/68)
GLINKA			
Russlan and Ludmilla: overture	LPO	ST 665	(6/67)
GLUCK			
Alceste: overture	BBCSO	DB 3129	(6/37)
GOUNOD			
O Divine Redeemer	Flagstad		
	LPO	LXT 5392	(12/58)
GRAINGER			
Over the Hills and Far Away	LPO	SRCS 71	(4/78)
GRIEG			
Piano Concerto	Cherkassky		
	LPO	ST 559	(3/66)

HANDEL

Acis and Galatea	Sutherland, Pears, Brannigan etc.		
	PHI	SOL 60011-2	(3/60)
Judas Maccabeus: Father of Heaven	Ferrier		
	LPO	LXT 5382	(2/53)
Messiah	Vyvyan, Procter, Maran,		
	Brannigan, LPC, LPO		
		LXT 2921-24	(5/54)
	Sutherland, Bumbry, McKellar,		
	Ward, LSC, LSO		
		SET 218-20	(11/61)
Messiah: He Was Despised and	Ferrier		
O Thou that Tellest	LPO	LXT 5382	(2/53)
Royal Fireworks Music	LPO	DB 2968-70	(12/49)
Organ Concertos op. 4 Nos. 1-6	Power Biggs		
	LPO	SABL 3260-1	(12/60)
Organ Concertos op. 7 Nos. 1-6	Power Biggs		
	LPO	SABL 3326-27	(12/60)
Samson: Return O God of Hosts	Ferrier		
	LPO	LXT 5382	(2/53)
Water Music	PPO	NCL 16017	(12/56)
Overture in D minor arr. Elgar	LPO	ASD 2822	(9/72)

HAYDN

German Dances Nos. 1, 6 and 7	LPO	HLP 19	(10/59)
Symphony No. 104	LPO	X 86	(?)

HINDEMITH

Symphony in E flat	LPO	SDBR 3008	(5/68)
Trauermusik	BroSO	P 142 L	(8/64)

HOLST

Beni Mora	LPO	SRCS 56	(5/72)
Choral Symphony	Palmer, LPC,		
	LPO	SAN 354	(10/74)
Egdon Heath	LPO	SXL 6006	(9/62)
Fugal Overture	LPO	SRCS 37	(10/68)
Hammersmith Prelude and Scherzo	LPO	SRCS 56	(5/72)
Hymn of Jesus	BBCC&SO	SXL 6006	(9/62)
Japanese Suite	LSO	SRCS 50	(6/11)
The Perfect Fool	LPO	LXT 5015	(4/55)
	LPO	SXL 6006	(9/62)
The Planets	BBCSO	DB 6227-33	(7/45)
	VOO	WHS 2033	(1/61)
	PPO	NLP 903	(6/54)
	NPO	ASD 2301	(3/67)
	LPO	ASD 3649	(4/79)
Λ Somerset Rhapsody	LPO	SRCS 56	(2/72)
Suite No. 1 orch. Jacob: march	LPO	SRCS 71	(4/78)

HOWELLS

Concerto for Strings	LPO	ASD 3020	(12/74)
Elegy for Viola and Strings	Downes		
	NPO	SRCS 69	(1/76)
Merry Eye	NPO	SRCS 69	(1/76)
Music for a Prince	NPO	SRCS 69	(1/76)
Processional	LPO	SRCS 71	(4/78)

HUMPERDINCK

Hansel and Gretel: overture	BrSO	D 591	(7/27)
	BBCSO	DB 1758	(12/32)

IRELAND

Concertino Pastorale	LPO	SRCS 31	(9/66)
Downland Suite: Elegy, Minuet	LPO	SRCS 31	(9/66)
Epic March	LPO	SRCS 31	(9/66)
The Forgotten Rite	LPO	SRCS 32	(9/66)
The Holy Boy	LPO	SRCS 31	(9/66)
Legend	Parkin		
	LPO	SRCS 32	(9/66)
London Overture	LPO	SRCS 31	(9/66)
Mai-Dun	LPO	SRCS 32	(9/66)
The Overlanders	LPO	SRCS 45	(2/71)
Piano Concerto	Parkin		
	LPO	SRCS 36	(10/68)
Satyricon	LPO	SRCS 32	(9/66)
Scherzo and Cortege from 'Julius			
Caesar'	LPO	SRCS 45	(2/71)
These Things Shall Be	Carol Case		
	LPO	SRCS 36	(10/68)
Tritons	LPO	SRCS 45	(2/71)

KHATCHATURIAN

Piano Concerto	Katz		
	LPO	CCL 30151	(4/59)

LALO

Cello Concerto	Nelsova		
	LPO	LXT 2906	(4/54)

LIDDLE

Abide with me	Flagstad		
	LPO	LXT 5392	(12/58)

LISZT

Fantasia on Hungarian Folktunes	Farnadi		
	PPO	WLAB 7018	(6/59)
Piano Concerto No. 1: 3rd movt	Tyrer		
	BrSO	ZPR 123	(cylinder rec.)
Totentanz	Farnadi		
	PPO	WLAB 7018	(6/59)

LITOLFF

Concerto Symphonique: scherzo	Curzon		
	LPO	SXL 2173	(2/60)
	Cherkassky		
	LPO	MFP 57004	(?)

MAHLER

Kindertotenlieder	Ludwig		
	PO	33CX 1671	(11/59)
	Flagstad		
	VPO	LXT 5395	(9/60)
Lieder Eines Fahrenden Gesellen	Flagstad		
	VPO	LXT 5395	(9/60)
Symphony No. 1	LPO	CM 31	(?)

MENDELSSOHN

The Hebrides	BBCSO	DB 2100	(4/34)
A Midsummer Night's Dream:			
Overture	BBCSO	DB 6242-43	(12/45)
	PPO	NCT 17009	(11/57)
Scherzo	PPO	NCT 17009	(11/57)
Intermezzo	PPO	NCT 17009	(11/57)
Nocturne	BBCSO	DA 1318	(8/33)
	PPO	NCT 17009	(11/57)
Wedding March	BBCSO	DB 6243	(12/45)
	PPO	NCT 17009	(11/57)
Dance of the Clowns	PPO	NCT 17009	(11/57)
Fairies' March	PPO	NCT 17009	(11/57)
Ruy Blas: overture	BBCSO	DB 2365	(1/35)
Symphony No. 3	PPO	NCL 16005	(8/58)
Symphony No. 4	PPO	NCL 16005	(8/58)
	LPO	ST 680	(3/68)
Violin Concerto	Rabin		
	PO	33CX 1597	(11/58)
	Menuhin		
	PO	ALP 1085	(11/53)
	Smith		
	LPO	ST 680	(3/68)
	Campoli		
	LPO	SXL 2026	(9/59)

MEYERBEER

Le Prophète: Coronation March	BBCSO	DB 1163	(5/37)

MOERAN

Cello Concerto	Coetmore		
	LPO	SRCS 43	(7/70)
Overture for a Masque	LPO	SRCS 43	(7/70)
Rhapsody No. 2	LPO	SRCS 43	(7/70)
Sinfonietta	LPO	SRCS 37	(10/68)

Symphony	NPO	SRCS 70	(7/75)

MONN

Cello Concerto: 1st movt	Pleeth		
	LPO	HLP 19	(10/57)

MOZART

Concerto for 2 pianos K.365	A. Schnabel, K.-U. Schnabel		
	LSO	DB 3033-35	(1/37)
Così fan tutte: overture	BBCSO	DB 2190	(7/34)
	BBCSO	DB 3814	(7/39)
Horn Concerto No. 3	A. Brain		
	BBCSO	DB 3973-74	(8/40)
Piano Concerto No. 17	Previn		
	LSO	ASD 2951	(1/74)
Piano Concerto No. 20	A. Fischer		
	PO	33CX 1686	(5/60)
Piano Concerto No. 23	A. Fischer		
	PO	33CX 1686	(5/60)
Piano Concerto No. 24	Previn		
	LSO	ASD 2951	(1/74)
Der Schauspieldirektor: overture	BBCSO	DB 1969	(4/34)
Symphony No. 32	BBCSO	DB 6172	(9/44)
Symphony No. 35	LPO	ASD 3158	(3/76)
Symphony No. 41	BBCSO	DB 1966-69	(4/34)
	LPO	ASD 3158	(3/76)
Die Zauberflöte: overture	LPO	ST 730	(7/68)

NICOLAI

The Merry Wives of Windsor: overture	BBCSO	DB 2195	(6/34)
	LPO	DB 21223	(3/51)

PAGANINI

Violin Concerto No. 1	Menuhin		
	LPO	ALP 1350	(11/56)

PARRY

The Birds: march	LPO	SRCS 71	(4/78)
Blest Pair of Sirens	LSO	C 3820-21	(12/48)
	LPC, LPO	ASD 2311	(5/67)
Elegy for Brahms	LPO	ASD 3725	(11/79)
English Suite	LSO	SRCS 48	(2/71)
Jerusalem	Flagstad		
	LPO	LXT 5392	(12/58)
Lady Radnor's Suite	LSO	SRCS 48	(2/71)
Overture to an Unwritten Tragedy	LSO	SRCS 48	(2/71)
Symphonic Variations	LSO	SRCS 48	(2/71)
	LPO	ASD 3725	(11/79)
Symphony No. 5	LPO	ASD 3725	(11/79)

PONCHIELLI

La Gioconda: Dance of the Hours	LPO	ST 730	(7/68)

PROKOFIEV

Lieutenant Kijé: suite	PCO	LXT 5119	(5/56)
The Love of Three Oranges: suite	LPO	LXT 5119	(5/56)
Piano Concerto No. 1	Katz		
	LPO	CCL 3051	(4/59)

RACHMANINOV

Rhapsody on a Theme of Paganini	Katchen		
	LPO	LXT 5374	(9/54)
	Katchen		
	LPO	SXL 2176	(7/60)
Piano Concerto No. 1	Katin		
	LPO	SXL 2034	(6/59)
Piano Concerto No. 2	Curzon		
	LPO	LXT 5178	(6/56)
Symphony No. 2	LPO	RB 16026	(4/66)
Symphony No. 3	LPO	RB 16147	(7/59)

RAVEL

Tzigane	Rabin		
	PO	33CX 1597	(11/58)

RESPIGHI

Feste Romane	PPO	WLAB 7012	(4/59)
Rossiniana	PPO	WLAB 7012	(4/59)

RODGERS

Guadalcanal March	LPO	ST 750	(10/68)

ROSSINI/BRITTEN

Matinées Musicales	PPO	NCT 17008	(2/59)
Soirées Musicales	PPO	NCT 17008	(2/59)
march only	LPO	SRCS 71	(4/78)

RUBBRA

Symphony No. 7	LPO	SRCS 41	(7/70)

SAINT-SAENS

Cello Concerto No. 1	Nelsova		
	LPO	LXT 2906	(4/54)
Danse Macabre	LPO	ST 698	(5/68)
Samson et Delila: Bacchanale	BBCSO	DB 2077	(11/33)
Wedding Cake	LPO	ST 698	(5/68)

SARASATE

Zigeunerweisen	Bress		
	LPO	ST 728	(6/68)

SCARLATTI/TOMMASINI

Good-humoured Ladies	BrSO	D 571-3	(10/26)

SCHUBERT

Symphony No. 9	BBCSO	DB 2415-20	(4/35)
	LPO	NCL 16006	(1/57)
	LPO	ASD 2856	(12/72)

SCHUMANN

Manfred Overture	BBCSO	DB 2189-90	(7/34)

Piano Concerto	Cherkassky		
	LPO	ST 559	(?)
Symphony No. 1	PPO	NCT 17004	(10/57)
Symphony No. 2	PPO	NCT 17005	(11/57)
Symphony No. 3	PPO	NCT 17006	(7/57)
Symphony No. 4	PPO	NCT 17007	(7/57)
SEARLE			
Symphony No. 1	LPO	SXL 2232	(10/60)
SHOSTAKOVITCH			
Symphony No. 6	LPO	SDBR 3007	(12/67)
SIBELIUS			
The Bard	PPO	NCL 16023	(11/58)
En Saga	PPO	NCL 16023	(11/58)
Finlandia	PPO	NCL 16024	(11/58)
Lemminkainen's Return	PPO	NCL 16023	(11/58)
Night Ride and Sunrise	BBCSO	DB 2795-96	(8/36)
	PPO	NCL 16024	(11/58)
The Oceanides	BBCSO	DB 2797	(8/36)
	PPO	NCL 16024	(11/58)
Pohjola's Daughter	PPO	NCL 16023	(11/58)
Romance in C	BBCSO	DB 3972	(7/40)
The Swan of Tuonela	PPO	NCL 16023	(11/58)
Tapiola	PPO	NCL 16024	(11/58)
The Tempest: prelude	PPO	NCL 16024	(11/58)
Violin Concerto	Menuhin		
	LPO	ALP 1350	(11/56)
SIMPSON			
Symphony No. 1	LPO	BLP 1092	(4/57)
SMETANA			
The Bartered Bride: overture, polka,			
furiant, Dance of the Comedians	LPO	ST 665	(6/67)
Ma Vlast: Vltava	LPO	ST 665	(6/67)
SMYTH			
The Dance	LightSO	TPX 9275	(?)
Fête Galante: Minuet	LightSO	DB3762	(5/39)
Two French Folk Melodies	LightSO	DB 3762	(5/39)
SOUSA			
Marches: El Capitan; Liberty Bell;			
Stars and Stripes; Washington Post	LPO	ST 750	(10/68)
STAMITZ			
Symphony in E flat: 1st and 2nd			
movts	LPO	HLP 18	(10/57)
STANFORD			
Becket: march	LPO	SRCS 71	(4/78)
J. STRAUSS I			
Radetzky March	LPO	ST 730	(7/68)

STRAVINSKY

Circus Polka	LPO	ST 698	(5/68)

SUPPE

Boccaccio: overture	PPO	NCL 16012	(5/58)
Fatinitza: overture	PPO	NCL 16012	(5/58)
Light Cavalry: overture	PPO	NCL 16012	(5/58)
Morning, Noon and Night: overture	PPO	NCL 16012	(5/58)
Poet and Peasant: overture	PPO	NCL 16012	(5/58)
	LPO	ST 730	(7/68)
Die Schöne Galathea: overture	PPO	NCL 16012	(5/58)

TCHAIKOVSKY

Capriccio Italien	BBCSO	DB 3956-57	(5/40)
Concert Fantasia	Katin		
	LPO	SXL 2034	(6/59)
1812: overture	LPO	LXT 2696	(8/52)
	LPO	ST 683	(4/68)
Eugene Onegin: Polonaise	BBCSO	DB 3132	(7/37)
Hamlet	LPO	LXT 2696	(8/52)
Marche Slave	BBCSO	DB 3971	(7/40)
	LPO	ST 683	(4/68)
Piano Concerto No. 1	Badura-Skoda		
	PPO	NCL 16013	(7/56)
Romeo and Juliet	LPO	ST 683	(4/68)
Serenade in C	BBCSO	DB 3303-05	(4/40)
Suite No. 3	PCO	LXT 5099	(3/56)
	LPO	ASD 3135	(11/75)
Symphony No. 3	LPO	LXT 5297	(3/56)
Symphony No. 5	LPO	GSGL 10027	(11/60)
Symphony No. 6	LPO	GSGL 10036	(2/60)
Violin Concerto	Elman		
	LPO	LXT 2970	(12/54)
	Bress		
	LPO	ST 728	(6/68)

TEIKE

Old Comrades	LPO	ST 750	(10/68)

TELEMANN

Viola Concerto in G	Couling		
	BroSO	P 142 L	(8/64)

TOMLINSON

Passepied	BroSO	P 142 L	(8/64)

TRADITIONAL etc.

The Battle Hymn of the Republic	LPO	ST 750	(10/68)
The British Grenadiers	BBCSO	B 8553	(4/37)
	LPO	ST 750	(10/68)
The Coronation of Queen Elizabeth II (Sir Adrian Boult conducted much of the music)	CorC&O	ALP 1056-58	(7/53)

Jubilate	Flagstad		
	LPO	LXT 5392	(12/58)
Lillibulero	LPO	ST 750	(10/68)
O Come all ye Faithful	Flagstad		
	LPO	LXT 5392	(12/58)
Rule Britannia	BBCSO	B 8553	(4/37)
Silent Night	Flagstad		
	LPO	LXT 5392	(12/58

VAUGHAN WILLIAMS

Concerto for two pianos	Vronsky and Babin		
	LPO	ASD 2469	(9/69)
Concerto Grosso	LPO	ASD 3286	(11/76)
Dona Nobis Pacem	Armstrong, Carol Case, LPC, LPO		
		ASD 2962	(4/74)
English Folk Songs Suite *orch.*			
Jacob	VOO	WST 14111	(5/61)
	LPO	NLP 905	(7/54)
	LSO	ASD 2750	(11/71)
Fantasia on a theme by Thomas			
Tallis	BBCSO	DB 3958-59	(6/40)
	LPO	NLP 905	(7/54)
	VOO	WST 14111	(5/61)
	LPO	SRCS 41	(7/70)
	LPO	ASD 3286	(11/76)
Flos Campi	Primrose, BBCC, BBCSO		
		DB 6353-55	(8/47)
Greensleeves Fantasia	LPO	NLP 905	(7/54)
	LSO	ASD 2750	(11/71)
In the Fen Country	NPO	ASD 2193	(9/68)
Job	BBCSO	DB 6289-93	(6/46)
	LPO	LXT 2937	(8/54)
	LPO	SDBR 3019	(2/66)
	LSO	ASD 2673	(4/71)
The Lark Ascending	Pougnet		
	LPO	PMB 1003	(10/53)
	Bean		
	NPO	ASD 2329	(10/67)
Norfolk Rhapsody	LPO	NLP 905	(7/54)
	NPO	ASD 2375	(6/68)
Old King Cole	LPO	LW 5151	(4/55)
Partita	LPO	SXL 2207	(7/60)
	LPO	ASD 3286	(11/76)
Pilgrim's Progress	Soloists, LPC, LPO		
		SLS 959	(2/72)
Serenade to Music	Festival Choir and orch.		
		DA 7040-41	(7/51)
	Soloists		
	LPO	ASD 2538	(4/70)

Symphony No. 1 (A Sea Symphony)	Baillie, Cameron, LPC, LPO		
		LXT 2907-08	(5/54)
	Armstrong, Carol Case, LPC, LPO		
		SLS 780	(12/68)
Symphony No. 2 (A London			
Symphony)	LPO	LXT 2693	(9/52)
	LPO	ASD 2740	(10/71)
Symphony No. 3 (Pastoral	Ritchie		
Symphony)	LPO	LXT 2787	(7/53)
	Armstrong		
	NPO	ASD 2393	(9/68)
Symphony No. 4	LPO	LXT 2909	(4/54)
	NPO	ASD 2375	(6/68)
Symphony No. 5	LPO	LXT 2910	(4/54)
	LPO	ASD 2538	(4/70)
Symphony No. 6	LSO	C 3873-76	(7/49)
	LPO	LXT 2911	(4/54)
	NPO	ASD 2329	(10/67)
Symphony No. 7 (Sinfonia	Gielgud,		
Antartica)	Ritchie		
	LPO	LXT 2912	(5/54)
	Burrowes		
	LPO	ASD 2631	(11/70)
Symphony No. 8	LPO	SXL 2207	(7/60)
	LPO	ASD 2469	(9/69)
Symphony No. 9	LPO	SDBR 6006	(2/60)
	LPO	ASD 2581	(9/70)
Thanksgiving for Victory	LCS, LPO	PMB 1003	(10/53)
Toward the Unknown Region	LPC, LPO	ASD 2962	(4/74)
The Wasps: incidental music	LPO	LXT 2907	(5/54)
	LPO	SLS 780	(12/68)

WAGNER

Götterdämmerung: Dawn and Siegfried's Rhine Journey; Siegfried's Funeral Music	LPO	ASD 2934	(12/73)
Lohengrin: preludes to Acts 1 and 3	NPO	ASD 2812	(7/72)
Die Meistersinger: prelude	BBCSO	DB 1924	(11/33)
	NPO	ASD 2812	(7/72)
prelude to Act 3	NPO	ASD 2812	(7/72)
Parsifal: Good Friday Music	BBCSO	DB 1677	(6/33)
Good Friday Music etc.	LSO	ASD 3000	(9/74)
Siegfried: Forest Murmurs	LPO	ASD 2934	(12/73)
Siegfried Idyll	LSO	ASD 3000	(9/74)
Tannhäuser: prelude	NPO	ASD 2812	(7/72)
prelude to Act 3	LPO	ASD 2934	(12/73)
Tristan und Isolde: prelude	BBCSO	DB 1757	(5/33)
	NPO	ASD 2812	(7/72)

Die Walküre: Ride of the Valkyries	LPO	ASD 2934	(12/73)

J. F. WAGNER

Under the Double Eagle	LPO	ST 750	(10/68)

WALFORD DAVIES

RAF March Past	LPO	ST 750	(10/68)

WALTON

Belshazzar's Feast	Noble, LPC, LPO		
		NLP 904	(4/54)
Crown Imperial	BBCSO	DB 3164	(6/37)
	LPO	ASD 3388	(4/77)
Orb and Sceptre	LPO	ASD 3388	(4/77)
Portsmouth Point	BBCSO	DA 1540	(1/37)
Scapino	LPO	LXT 5028	(6/55)
	LPO	ST 698	(5/68)
Siesta	LPO	LXT 5028	(6/55)
Symphony No. 1	PPO	NCL 16020	(7/64)

WEBER

Euryanthe: overture	BBCSO	DB 3130	(7/37)
Der Freischütz: overture	BBCSO	DB 1678	(4/33)

WIENIAWSKI

Violin Concerto No. 1	Rabin		
	PO	33CX 1538	(6/58)
Violin Concerto No. 2	Elman		
	LPO	LXT 5222	(11/56)

WILLIAMSON

Violin Concerto	Menuhin		
	LPO	ASD 2759	(2/72)

WOLF

Italian Serenade	PO	7ER 5129	(4/59)

WOLF-FERRARI

The Jewels of the Madonna: Intermezzo	LPO	ST 730	(7/68)

ZIMMERMAN

Anchors Away	LPO	ST 750	(10/68)